THE
LAWYER
THE LION &
THE LAUNDRY

Three Hours to Finding Your
Calm in the Chaos

JAMIE JACKSON SPANNHAKE

Cover design by Mark Feldman & Briana Ball
Logo design by Briana Ball
Interior drawings by Jamie Jackson Spannhake

The content of this book is for general instruction only. Each person's physical, emotional, and spiritual condition is unique. The instruction in this book is not intended to replace or interrupt the reader's relationship with a physician or other professional. Please consult your doctor for matters pertaining to your own health.

To contact the publisher, visit
www.AttorneyatWork.com

To contact the author, visit
www.JamieSpannhake.com

Printed in the United States of America

ISBN-13: 978-1-7333736-1-6

First Printing: September 2019
Published by Attorney at Work, Lake Zurich, Illinois.
www.attorneyatwork.com

*This book is dedicated to all
the authors and teachers from
whom I have learned the lessons
that I synthesize and share in
this book, and to my friends and
family, especially Sarah, who
have allowed me to practice these
lessons imperfectly.*

CONTENTS

A NOTE FROM THE AUTHOR

Mark Twain is attributed with saying something like, "I wanted to write you a short letter, but I didn't have time." As Twain knew, it is time-consuming to condense ideas and weed out unnecessary material to get to the essence of the information.

I took the time to write a short book for you because we are all very busy with competing responsibilities. I want you to be able to read the entire book in about three hours so you can incorporate into your life the choices, actions, and thoughts I have learned and share. I hope they are as helpful to you as they have been for me.

PREFACE

I conceived of this book while on a yoga and meditation retreat with Cyndi Lee at Kripalu Yoga and Retreat Center in Stockbridge, Massachusetts. I had been thinking of writing it for a long time, but prior to that weekend, it was a jumble of thoughts without a definite form and mostly not usable to anyone but me. The idea was full of information, but disorganized. That weekend of quiet, meditation, breathing, healthy food, and exercise was this book in action. It allowed me to organize my thoughts, define a path, and start the journey of writing with intention and direction.

Part of this book arises directly from my experience of that weekend exploring how our choices and thoughts affect our lives. The tools and techniques in the "Choose" and "Think" sections allow you to define your personal values to determine what you really want your life to look like. I also explain the theories underlying mindfulness, explore the negative and unhelpful ways we think about our lives and time, and guide you through changing your mental habits.

The months that followed helped create the rest of this book, during which I determined to stay on the path I envisioned during my retreat at Kripalu, but often struggled to do so in the midst of the chaos that is life outside a weekend retreat. The tools and techniques in the "Act" section address changing your relationship with time and reclaiming time in each day by using your resources most effectively and efficiently.

Utilizing all the tools, tips, and techniques in this book will allow you to truly have the life you want. I urge you to read and work through each of the exercises so that, as you implement the tools and techniques, you can reach the place of balance and fulfillment that you desire: a place where you are living the life you deserve while feeling full of life and energy, not overwhelmed and exhausted.

If you are a busy person like me, who identifies as a professional, parent, daughter, and giver, you don't have a lot of time to read books and work through lengthy exercises. I understand. With that in mind, I've written a short book, one that you can read and work through in about three hours. Most importantly, *this book does not require you to add more to your busy schedule.* Rather, I'm sharing perspective shifts — two choices, two actions, and two thoughts — that allow you to create space and time to live the life you want.

There is a lot more that I want to share with you that is not included here. If you want more information and to work through the perspective shifts in a more guided way, use *The Lawyer, the Lion, & the Laundry Workbook*. It contains in-depth step-by-step guidance for all the exercises and questions in the book and offers daily practices to keep you on track. It is available at my website, www.JamieSpannhake.com. Also available is a deck of Practice Cards that will give you ideas to try each day.

In addition, the "References & Resources" section at the back of the book includes information on books, websites, apps, places, people, and other resources so you can dive deeper into any aspect you desire. You can use many of the resources to implement the different tools for reclaiming hours in your days.

There's more information, as well as regularly updated resources, at my website and blog at www.JamieSpannhake.com. See the "More" section at the back of this book as well.

As you read the book, keep this in mind: Although I am serious about life, I don't take myself too seriously. I've tried to infuse this book with humor. I find it helps everything if we lighten up a bit, especially when we laugh at ourselves!

I hope you will read and reread this book as many times as desired or needed, as life changes and as you change. Sometimes change can make you take a step back, or push the pause button, to reassess everything, including your goals, priorities, and expectations. The changes in my personal life while I was writing this book epitomize how we sometimes need to pause and reassess.

When I started this book, I was married and spent my mornings, before my husband and daughter awoke, writing. My days were filled with lawyering and mom-ing, but my early mornings were dedicated to writing. Then as we contemplated moving to another state so my husband could pursue his career with his then-current employer, my writing time fell away as we spent all our non-work time visiting new schools and neighborhoods. This book languished for months. When my husband took a new job so we would not be moving, I thought I would get back to this book. But another change: We decided to divorce. In the midst of house-hunting, divorce mediation, financial rearrangements, and emotional support for myself and my daughter, there was no time for writing. I was barely keeping my life and career intact in light of the great upheaval in our lives.

It took a year to reach a new kind of normal before I could get back to writing. But I did. I practiced the choices, actions, and thoughts I advocate in the following pages. I made deliberate choices to live my values even when times were tough. I continued to take actions that helped me. And I managed my thoughts to more effectively manage my life. Because the path I had created for myself was clear and well-defined, it was easier to stay on track.

No matter the changes and challenges you face in your life, remember: The life you desire requires practice, but perfection is not required.

You can find joy in the imperfect journey.

INTRODUCTION

I've always been that person who does a lot, all at the same time. People have often said to me, "I don't know how you have time to do all that!" So, back in 2008, I started thinking about why that is. What do I do differently that enables me to handle many things at the same time? That's when I started presenting and writing about time management. As time went on, I realized that I had lots of tools, techniques, and tips that enabled me to manage many different aspects of life simultaneously.

Indeed, I was managing it all: daily life, career, family, and social life. But I was so busy that I felt overwhelmed and exhausted. I wasn't enjoying my life. That's when I realized that time management tools alone are not sufficient for a successful *and enjoyable life*. I needed some kind of "mind management" as well — a way to approach things differently to prevent losing my mind. That's when I discovered mindfulness and meditation; I'd discovered a better way.

This book is what I've learned and practiced. Through these choices, actions, and thoughts, I enjoy my life despite my numerous responsibilities and activities. I have a wonderful and happy eight-year-old daughter. My ex-husband and I have an amicable and successful co-parenting relationship. I take care of my daughter, two dogs, two cats, myself, foster kids, a law and mediation practice, a freelance writing career, and I'm partially responsible for my aging parents. Even with these responsibilities, I still have time to volunteer at my daughter's school, regularly practice yoga and meditation, play tennis, and run several miles three to four times each week.

Maybe that sounds like too much to you. Or maybe it sounds like the easy life because you have many more responsibilities than I do. Either way, it's about how you perceive and feel about your days, not whether your days are more or less busy than the next person. Even if my life doesn't sound like the perfect balance to you, the perspective shifts I've learned and share in this book will guide you to finding what works for you. I want you to have all that you want in your life; I want you to enjoy your days.

Why should you listen to me? I've lived it. I've researched, read books and articles, attended workshops, and talked to innumerable people about what works for them. I've tried lots of different tools and techniques over the past 10 years, experimenting in my own life. Sometimes, I've failed miserably. Other times, I've been very successful. I've done the testing for you and found what works. You can benefit from my mistakes without making them yourself.

Also, I am certified as a health coach, so I have a base of knowledge regarding wellness that informs the information in this book.

In creating the perspective shifts and exercises, I've synthesized a wealth of information and distilled theories into clear, easy-to-use applications for you.

Join me for a fun and enlightening journey to learn how to CHOOSE (in Part 1), ACT (in Part 2), and THINK (in Part 3) in ways that will clarify your desires so you can reclaim your time and enjoy your life. All you need is an open mind and an investment of about three hours of focused energy.

Let's get started!

PART 1

CHOOSE

Habits are learned. Choose them wisely.
– Thomas M. Sterner

Peace.
It does not mean to be in a place
where there is no noise, trouble, or hard work.
It means to be in the midst of those things
and still be calm in your heart.
– Unknown

CHOOSE
WHAT YOU WANT

Most people never get what they want
because they don't ask for it.
– Madonna

It's not about having it all.
It's about having what you value most.
– Jean Chatzky

No one actually wants it all.
We simply want what matters to us.
– Kate Northrup

The best life is the intentional and deliberate life: a life where you take the time to thoughtfully decide how you want your life to be. For this best life, we need to take into account all aspects of ourselves and our lives to ensure that we feel happy, fulfilled, and content. In this chapter, you'll get the opportunity to choose what you really want your life to be like. It's crucial to spend the time assessing your values — not just your goals — to ensure that after you work diligently to create the life you desire, you don't wind up feeling empty and overwhelmed.

My Story: Be Careful What You Work For, You Just Might Get It

After unsuccessfully pursuing an acting career in my early 20s, I decided to change my life dramatically. I walked away from the arts without a backward glance, and jumped headfirst into law school. I had been working the third shift (midnight to 8:00 a.m.) in a large Manhattan law firm in the document production department. Lawyers would bring their marked-up documents — legal briefs, court papers, transaction agreements — to the document production department before they left for the evening. We would make all the changes so the documents would be ready for the lawyers when they returned to the office in the morning. It was a world that I was beginning to see from the inside. I felt I could be a good lawyer. So, I became one.

I worked hard in law school and loved every minute of it. I loved the logical reasoning, problem-solving, identifying issues, advocating for a position, and writing. I was good at it, too. It was like I was born to be a lawyer. My brain naturally worked the way it needed to work in order to do well in that environment.

I graduated magna cum laude and received a job offer from a large law firm in Manhattan. I was thrilled. This was the prestigious position that I envisioned for myself. I was going to be like one of the lawyers I saw when I was working in the document production department. I went in full force and it was great ... for about six months. By then I realized that the values in the firm were not my values — something that became abundantly clear to me on my birthday.

I had invited my four closest friends to a dinner party at my apartment that evening, a Friday. I had planned to leave work around 5:30 p.m. to get home and start cooking. I was still at the office at 6:30, with my friends expected to arrive at 7:00. I went to the partner with whom I was working and told him about the plans I had for my birthday, and asked if I could head out. He put his pen down, perturbed. With a dramatic sigh and an unhappy face, he said, "Be back early tomorrow morning, by 8:00. See you then." Then he went back to work. "Tomorrow" was Saturday.

He didn't wish me a happy birthday. He didn't suggest that I take the weekend off to relax or do something enjoyable. That was my first indication that perhaps I had worked really hard to achieve something I didn't actually want.

Six years later, I was still practicing law in Manhattan. I had switched firms and was working with a mentor whose values were more closely aligned with mine: namely, a belief that I was not just a lawyer, but also a person with interests other than my career. Unfortunately, the majority of the lawyers, and especially the firm leadership, were not so "balanced." Still, I was on "partnership track," working toward the goal that everyone in the firm wanted: to be asked to join the partnership. Then, one day I heard an analogy that changed everything: Becoming partner in a large law firm is like winning a pie-eating contest where the prize is more pie. I realized that, if I didn't enjoy the value system in the firm when I was on the periphery as an associate, I would like it even less when I was enmeshed in it as a partner.

For me, the analogy was more accurately stated as: Becoming partner would be like winning a pie-eating contest where the prize is more pie ... *and I don't even like pie!*

Holy crap! What had I done? I had spent all that time, effort, and money to achieve great success at something I didn't even like.

My mistake was that I didn't take the time to determine my values, what was important to me, and what I truly wanted before I started down the long path to law firm partnership. You can learn from my mistake by carefully considering the questions and exercises in this chapter so that you have a vision of what you want your life to be. That way, when you arrive at the place that is your success, you actually enjoy it.

If I had taken the time to more carefully assess what I wanted my life to look like, I could have made different choices in law school. Those choices would have given me the contacts and experiences earlier on to create a law career that actually works for me — like the one I have now. Today I am a partner in a small law firm with five partners, and we all have families and interests outside the law. We work very hard, within a value system that makes sense to me. I got here eventually, but the path was longer and more difficult than it needed to be.

What Do You Want in Your Life?

Take some time, as much as you need — minutes, hours, or days — to really think about what you want in your life. Consider what you want your life to look like. Depending on where you are in your life, you may envision it differently. You can tweak this definition as much or as often as you need, as thoughts, goals, and circumstances change over time, so do not feel that this is your one and only opportunity. However, keep in mind that while goals may change, values are usually consistent throughout life, even as circumstances change.

Consider the "Big Picture"

Consider the life you imagined for yourself: all the different aspects, people, and places. Here are some helpful starter questions to get you going. Write down your answers, preferably in a journal or in *The Lawyer, the Lion, & the Laundry Workbook* (available at www.JamieSpannhake.com), so you can easily go back to them as needed.

1. What kind of person do you want to be?

2. What kind of parent, child, sibling, or spouse do you want to be?

3. What kind of physical environment do you want to live in?

4. What kind of people do you want around you?

5. Do you want a family? What does "family" mean to you? Having a partner? Children? Pets?

6. Do you want to work outside the home? Do you want a "career"? What does that mean to you? What does it look like?

7. What does financial stability look like to you?

8. What activities are important to you? What activities do you enjoy?

9. What kind of spiritual or religious practice is meaningful to you, if any?

10. What kind of community do you want to live and participate in?

Ask as many questions as you need to define what you want. Try to focus on creating a positive picture of your life. Some people find it easier to consider what they don't want in order to define what they do want, but you'll do that in your next step when you consider what is lacking in your life. For now, focus on what you want.

If you prefer, create a visual mind map of the life you desire — a positive mind map. Check out Mind Meister for its mind mapping tool online and via its app (www.MindMeister.com). For more information, see the "Resources" section.

I include my answers to the questions and my mind map here so you can see samples. But don't be swayed by my thoughts; my desired life may not be what's right for you.

WHAT IS MIND MAPPING?

Mind mapping is a representation of ideas, thoughts, and concepts in a graphical way. It can have the same purpose as linear list-making, journaling with words, contemplation of solutions, and analytical thinking.

Why use mind mapping?

The benefit of mind mapping is that it is not only analytical, but also artistic. It engages more parts of your brain than list-making and other linear ways of thinking. By engaging the artistic parts of your brain (and everyone has artistic parts of the brain, not just artists!), you can reach more creative solutions and ideas. Plus, it is fun!

How to mind map

As easy as 1, 2, 3:

1. **Start in the middle of the page and create a shape, maybe a circle, to contain the idea you want to analyze or develop.** Use words or pictures inside the shape to represent the idea.

2. **Create subtopics and parts of the central idea.** Around this central shape and its contents, create shapes and images, and perhaps add words, then connect those subtopics and parts with lines and shapes to the central shape.

3. **Create the parts of the subtopics around those shapes and images.** If appropriate, connect the subtopics to other subtopics, or break them down further.

There's a place for your mind maps in *The Lawyer, the Lion, & the Laundry Workbook.*

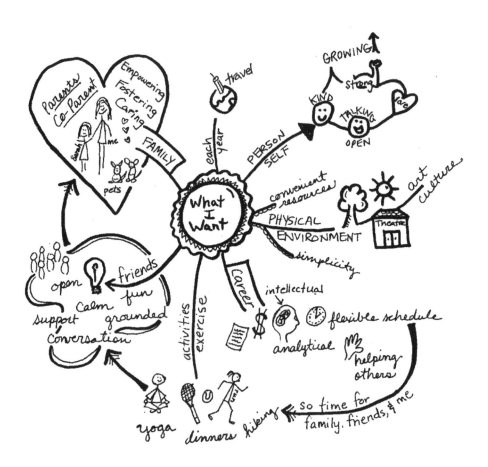

What I Want

1. What kind of person do I want to be?

    I want to be kind, compassionate, communicative, open-minded, strong, and loving.

2. What kind of parent, child, sibling, spouse do I want to be?

    I want to be understanding, compassionate, listening, respectful, helpful, supportive, with time to make one feel loved and important, and fun! A person who helps my loved ones help themselves so they feel empowered but also know that they can run to me for help when they need it. Unconditional love.

3. What kind of physical environment do I want to live in?

    I need nature and open space, but I also need resources and amenities within close distance. I want arts available to me, especially performing arts. I like quiet spaces. I need lots of light. I like for my living space to be uncluttered and things to be organized.

4. What kind of people do I want around me?

    I enjoy the company of intelligent people who have a sense of groundedness, practicality, and calm. I like people who are open to a spiritual practice and believe life is about more than what one can acquire or accomplish.

5. Do I want a family? What does "family" mean to me?

    Family is the most important thing. That includes parents, a spouse, and children. I'd like to have two children, but have been blessed with one amazing daughter and that is sufficient. I'd like to have a loving relationship with my sister, too. And pets are an important part of our family. I always want cuddly pets.

6. Do I want to work outside the home? Do I want a "career"? What does that mean to me? What does it look like?

    I want a career. Something that pays well and that is interesting, at least some of the time. Flexibility and autonomy are important to me, so deadline-driven, self-motivated work is best for me. I like writing, problem-solving, analytical thinking, strategizing, organizing, and helping others, especially in a mentoring relationship. I love to learn new things.

7. What does financial stability look like to me?

Having everything I need and some things I want. I like to know that I can cover all my necessities and some wants without considering a budget. I want to be able to travel, at least one vacation each year, and to visit family and friends without major financial planning. I don't need fancy things, but I like nice things. Think Toyota instead of Mercedes, swim club instead of country club, Ann Taylor instead of Brooks Brothers.

8. What activities are important to me? What activities do I enjoy?

A regular yoga practice; a regular meditation practice; tennis, at least once each week; walking the dogs, including hikes in the woods; running regularly; performing arts and seeing or being in a show a few times each year; dinners with friends, at home or restaurants; seeing and experiencing nature, especially animals; truthful and thoughtful conversation with intelligent and interesting people; time to rejuvenate on a monthly basis.

9. What kind of spiritual or religious practice is meaningful to me, if any?

Mindfulness meditation with Buddhist beliefs that inform the way I live my life and approach all things.

10. In what kind of community do I want to live and participate?

A tolerant community of peace-loving people. I want a network of people that I can rely on to help and support me, and I will do the same for them. I want a community that makes being healthy and kind easier, not harder. I'd like access to good, healthy food. I'd like to see other people being active and exercising so that it is the norm and easier for me to do the same.

If you haven't answered these questions for yourself, do so now. It is an investment of time with a significant return. You can write your answers and draw your mind map in your journal or in the *Workbook*.

What's Missing in Your Life?

Now that you know what you want, or are at least on the path to learning what you want your life to look like, let's explore what's missing in your life.

Pema Chödrön, who is a Buddhist teacher and a mom, explains that we think we need certain things to change in order for our lives to be better. She gives an example in one of her books: "If it weren't for my husband, I'd have a perfect marriage."

That's the way we approach so many things:

- If only I had more money, I'd be happy.
- If only my kids just listened to me, my life would be calmer.
- If only my boss were different, my job would be great.
- If only my tummy were flatter, I'd feel fabulous.

Let's go there together now. What's missing? What's wrong? We'll talk about whether you can or need to change these things in Part 3, "Think," where you will learn how to work with your perceived negatives instead of against them. Approach this exercise with laughter.

Here's part of my list:

- If only I lived closer to my daughter's school, my life would be easier.
- If only I lived closer to my parents and sister, my life would be better.
- If only I had another child, my daughter would be happier.
- If only I had more money, I could have more fun.
- If only I had more money, I could work less and have less stress.

You get the idea. Another way to find your "problems" is to fill in the blank:

If only I had _____, then life would be the way I want.

If only I had a housekeeper. If only I had a nanny. If only I had a more helpful spouse. If only I had a cook. If only I had someone to do my laundry. If only I had time to exercise daily. If only I had more time, then I'd be happier.

Again, we'll focus on what to do about these "problems" later. For now, just get them all out on paper, either in a linear list or a visual representation. There's a place to write your list and draw your mind map in the *Workbook*. Below is an example where I added these perceived negatives to my original positive mind map.

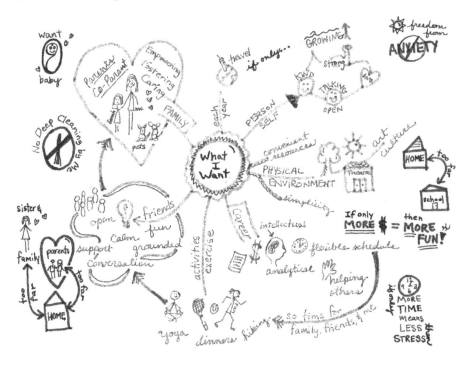

Your Values Statement

Examining the answers to your questions and thoughts about what you want and what is lacking in your life will help you develop an understanding of your values so you can clearly define what you *really* want. If it would be helpful, write out or draw a "values statement" for your life. Your values statement could be one paragraph that succinctly encapsulates the information you have learned through defining what you want and what is lacking. Or, you can simply review your answers and information to ensure that your values are clear in your mind. Or, if you are a visual person, you can create a vision board. Whatever method you use, you are creating the framework for your life.

Think About the Details

You now have the beginnings of a framework for your life based on your values. You know what you want and what you don't want. Next, let's consider the details of what you want — in other words, how you want to actually spend the hours in your days.

When I think about the details of my life, these are some of the things I want, in no particular order:

- Quality time with my daughter every day
- Regular nights out, maybe twice a month
- Exercise five days a week
- Write every day for an hour
- Eat homemade nutritious and delicious food most of the time
- Successful legal career
- Regular yoga practice
- Regular meditation practice
- Run at least seven miles each week
- Clean and neat house
- Clean laundry
- Stylish clothes
- Time with friends
- Daily hikes with my dogs
- Yearly vacation to interesting and culturally different locations
- Play tennis at least once a week
- Trip to NYC to see a Broadway show once a month
- Clean car
- Get eight hours of sleep each night

Referring to the framework of your life, write down your own details in your journal or in the *Workbook* — the specifics of what you want in your life.

Quantifying Your Time

Contemplating your wants and needs is a helpful exercise, but too often that's where it ends. Turning them into reality requires planning, determination, and, possibly, some difficult shifts in perspective. First, you need to quantify the time needed on a monthly basis for all the things you want. This means determining how much time you either want to spend on them or how much time they require. For example, here is the list I created, quantified by assigning an amount of time to each item. I've also created a visual mind map of my time. For items that occur weekly (like exercise), I've listed the number of hours needed each week, then multiplied by 4 to calculate the approximate monthly hours.

My Time List

- Quality time with my daughter every day: 40 hours per week x 4 = 160

- Exercise 5 days a week for 30 minutes: 2.5 hours per week x 4 = 10

- Daily hikes with my dogs: 5 hours per week x 4 = 20

- Write every day for an hour: 7 hours per week x 4 = 28

- Eat homemade nutritious and delicious food most of the time: 15 hours per week x 4 = 60

- Successful legal career: 30 hours per week x 4 = 120

- Regular yoga practice (twice a week): 5 hours per week x 4 = 20

- Regular meditation practice: 2 hours per week x 4 = 8

- Run at least 7 miles each week: 1.5 hours per week x 4 = 6

- Clean and neat house: 3 hours per week x 4 = 12

- Clean laundry: 4 hours per week x 4 = 16

- Time with friends: 7 hours per week x 4 = 28

- Play tennis at least once a week: 2 hours per week x 4 = 8

- Clean car: 1 hour per week x 4 = 4

- Get 8 hours of sleep each night: 56 hours per week x 4 = 224

- Volunteer, mostly at my daughter's school: 2 hours per week x 4 = 8

- Stylish clothes: shopping and/or dry-cleaning time: 2 hours per month

- Regular night out, twice a month: 8 hours per month

- Trip to NYC to see a Broadway show once a month: 12 hours per month

- Yearly vacation to interesting and culturally different locations: time to plan and travel: 2 weeks every year*

  This will require that I not do many of the other things on the list, so I'm not going to factor it in to my regular time; rather, when the time comes to plan and go on vacation, I'll put some of the other items "on hold."

TOTAL HOURS NEEDED PER MONTH: 754 HOURS

MY VISUAL TIME

Now you do the same: Quantify the items on your list or mind map.

Reality Check

When I look at the details of my time, it's clear that I would need more than 24 hours in a day and more than 365 days in a year to actually do all that I want.

Since there are approximately 720 hours in a month, at 754 monthly hours to do all the things I want, I would need an extra 34 hours each month. That is more than a full extra day. And the preceding calculations do not take into account all those unexpected things that life brings: sick kids, emergency meetings with clients, car repairs, broken washing machine, snowstorms, school delays, and so on. My expectations are unrealistic. I've set myself up to fail, no matter how hard I try.

This is an important exercise. You may be beating yourself up because you never achieve all that you set out to do. But maybe you are setting the bar at an impossible level. It's like saying "I'm going to feel bad about myself if I don't live *every 30 hours of each day to the fullest!*" Of course you will fail because it is impossible.

To be clear, I am not asking you to lower your expectations; I am proposing that you need realistic expectations.

Adjust Your Expectations: The Three B's

What to do? My dear friend Tal Fagin, who is a Martha Beck-trained life coach, uses a tool called "The Three B's." The B's are "Bag It, Barter It, Better It."

When you think about the items on your lists up to this point, of all the things you want to accomplish, ask yourself the following questions.

1. *Can you "Bag It," that is, can you just not do it?* There may be consequences here, so you need to consider those. If you are OK with the consequences, then maybe you can just not do it. Take, for example, my desire for a clean and neat house. I need a neat house to not feel overwhelmed by clutter, which causes me anxiety and makes it more difficult to handle life. But I can "bag" a really clean house. I have two dogs and two cats, so with all the fur, I would need to vacuum every day to keep the house truly clean. But I don't, because I don't want to spend my time vacuuming. Instead, I have a house cleaner come every two weeks to thoroughly clean. I can deal with the consequence of dog fur and have decided to "bag" my desire for an always-clean house.

2. *Can you "Barter It," that is, delegate it or have someone else do it for you?*
   While true bartering does not include payment of money for services, in this
   case, include that option. If you can pay someone to do any of the things on
   your list, or take turns with someone, or even buy a product, to keep the
   benefit but not spend the time, then you are bartering it. Good examples of
   activities you can "barter" are shopping for clothes by using a service like
   Stitch Fix, preparing meals by using a service like HelloFresh, cleaning by
   hiring a housekeeper, and transporting your kids to and from school and
   after-school activities by partnering with another parent. I use all these.
   Others ways to barter include letting teenagers use Lyft or Uber to get to
   and from after-school or weekend activities. And, one that I haven't tried
   yet, but that sounds fabulous is a Neato robot to vacuum the floor every day
   so the dog fur doesn't linger between cleanings!

3. *Can you "Better It"?* Some things *must* be done only by you, so can you
   create a way that works better for you? My example of this is getting up early
   to write or work. I like to be up early, in a quiet house and able to watch the
   sunrise, with the ability to accomplish things that are important to me before
   anyone else in the house is awake. But actually getting up early I do not enjoy.
   So, I "bettered" it. I love good coffee in the morning, so I bought a new coffee
   pot with a timer. I set the coffee to start brewing at the same time my alarm
   goes off. When I wake, I can smell the coffee and it makes the morning just
   a bit "better," which gives me that little incentive to get up. Once I'm up and
   drinking my coffee, I'm happy to be up. Little things like this can make a big
   difference. One could say, without my new coffee pot, I would never have
   written this book!

Apply the Three B's to Your List

Go through your list of wants and needs and ask "The Three B's" for each item.
Now you are on track to setting realistic expectations. Keep doing the three
B's and adjusting the details and time required until you have defined a daily,
weekly, and monthly life that is possible for you to achieve. If you'd like more
guidance for applying the three B's and creating realistic expectations, refer to
the *Workbook.*

In the next chapter, you will learn how to choose which thoughts to follow,
rather than letting your mind take you away. This will be the practice of mindfulness, which will help settle your mind to make your priorities clearer. After you
develop your mindfulness practice, you may want to refine your values and goals
by reworking your framework and details using the exercises in this chapter.

A Word About Your Job

"Work-life balance" is a phrase used a lot to describe what you are trying to attain by clarifying your values. I think the phrase is *almost* right, but I prefer to call it "work-life integration" because that better describes the way it works: We integrate all our priorities into our lives. This integration of personal and professional life requires focus, commitment, and energy, as well as the courage to pave your own way sometimes, especially in the face of people who don't get it.

According to The Work Foundation, "Work-life balance is about people having a measure of control over when, where and how they work. It is achieved when an individual's right to a fulfilled life inside and outside paid work is accepted and respected as the norm, to the mutual benefit of the individual, business and society."

One of the things I like about this definition is it makes clear that balance benefits everyone. More importantly, though, when we look at this definition, we realize that for "work-life balance" to be achieved, the values systems of *both* the employee and the employer must enable fulfillment inside and outside of work. Individually, many of us are achieving this. Some companies and firms understand it as well. But not every employer makes it easy or possible for their employees to achieve some kind of balance or integration.

When I was a senior associate at a large Manhattan law firm, my priorities became clear to me. I wanted to be a lawyer, but I also wanted to be a wife, mother, daughter, and friend. Once my priorities were clear, I realized I had to change my employment situation. I opted to reduce my schedule to part-time rather than leave my job. I liked my job but didn't want to work 50-plus hours a week. In that context, working part-time meant *only* 40 hours a week. I talked with my mentor about this, and he was supportive. He knew I wanted to start a family and that I had recently moved out of Manhattan in search of a more tranquil lifestyle. With his support, I approached the chair of the litigation department in which I worked. As part of our discussion, the chair said I needed to understand that switching to a part-time track meant that I would never be considered for partner because the desire to work part-time brought into question my dedication to the law. WTF! In the value system of the firm, if I wanted to be a lawyer, I could *only* be a lawyer.

After considering the consequences, I switched to a part-time schedule. I decided to live within *my* value system, not someone else's. This also meant that it was now inevitable that I had to plan my exit strategy.

When the time came to leave, it wasn't easy to give up the "golden handcuffs" of the law firm. The salary was tremendous, as was the prestige. But two years after switching to part-time work, I was able to make my exit. I also was able to get pregnant and have a baby, which took three rounds of in vitro fertilization to accomplish. Almost three years after leaving the firm, when my daughter was 18 months old, I was able to start my own law practice, one that was built on my values, working part-time and tailored to her schedule. Three years later, I had the opportunity to bring my practice to a small law firm with other lawyers who shared my values. Now, finally, I am a lawyer, a mother, a daughter, and a friend. I have my work-life integration, but it would not have been possible without changing my job and career trajectory.

I am not necessarily suggesting that you leave your employment situation, but if your job makes it impossible for you to live your values, you may need to readjust your values or adjust your employment in some way — perhaps by changing your role, reducing your schedule, or hiring an experienced assistant. Or maybe you need a new job. There are insightful questions in the *Workbook* to help you assess how your values and your job align or not.

DETOX YOUR CONTACTS TO BETTER YOUR LIFE

Assess whether the people in your life make it more difficult to have the life you want. Do they take more than their share of your resources — late-night calls, impossible to please, extreme lateness and repeated last-minute cancellations, or constant "fire drills"? Think about what your life would be like without those people. How could you use those same resources to improve your life, your attitude, and your time? It might be worth it to end a relationship in order to better use your resources for yourself and other people who do not monopolize your time and energy, or compromise your sanity.

"Choose What You Want" Review

1. Determine what you want in your life.

2. Determine what, if anything, is currently missing in your life.

3. Adjust your expectations to be realistic about what is possible in the amount of time you have.

4. Consider how your values compare with the values of those around you, especially in your career.

5. As you, your life, and your circumstances change, revisit this chapter to tweak your values and goals to ensure that they continue to work for you.

CHOOSE WHICH THOUGHTS TO FOLLOW

The greatest weapon against stress is our ability
to choose one thought over another.
– William James

There is one thing you can do each day that will greatly improve your life, health, and relationships. You can do it anywhere. It doesn't cost anything. It doesn't require special tools or skills. And it only takes a minimum of five minutes each day. It is mindfulness through meditation.

Mindfulness and Meditation

Mindfulness means being present in the moment and focusing on what is happening *right now*. The opposite would be distractedness; for instance, while at work, you're focusing on all the things that need to be done at home, or vice versa. Meditation can be used to develop and practice mindfulness. When you practice mindfulness, you engage in deliberate actions (or inactions) that are intentional and conscious and less reactive.

The Lion vs. The Dog

There is a story about a lion, a dog, and a bone. Imagine that you have a bone in your hand. Sitting across from you is a dog. As you wave the bone around, the dog follows every movement of the bone. The dog may not even notice you; instead, he is focused on the bone. You move the bone left, his head moves in the same direction. You raise the bone over your head, the dog looks up. It's as if the dog cannot help himself; he must follow the bone. If you throw the bone in the corner, the dog will run after the bone without hesitation.

Now consider the same scenario, except rather than a dog, there is a lion sitting across from you. As you wave the bone around, the lion might notice the bone, but he also notices you. As you move the bone to the left, the lion might notice that you moved the bone, but more likely, he is focused on you. When you throw the bone into the corner, the lion is not likely to chase it. He may turn his head to the corner, but he chooses not to follow the bone.

The bone is an analogy for our thoughts. You want to be more like a lion and less like a dog. You want to choose which bones — thoughts — to follow, rather than chasing every bone you see — or thought you think. You want to remain focused on what is important to you, rather than chasing every thought that crosses your mind.

The Benefits

Mindfulness and meditation create calm and focus the mind, cultivating greater attention and clarity. Mindfulness is scientifically validated to help people deal with the challenges and stressors of life. By working on focus and attention, you can manage your emotions better, connect with others more successfully, and become happier and more effective in your work and life. It can change the way you deal with yourself, your stressors, other people, and life. Essentially, it allows you to remain calm in the midst of the storm, without letting circumstances overwhelm you and cause frustration and exhaustion. Mindful action is proactive rather than reactive.

For example, when my daughter refuses to take no for an answer, I get frustrated. When I am not practicing mindful action, I eventually lash out. It usually happens like this:

Me: No, you can't do that.

Sarah: Please, mommy, it will only take a few minutes.

Me: No, it is too late and I want you to get a good night's rest.

Sarah: Mommy, please, I really want to do it now.

Me: (Getting frustrated) Sarah, honey, it's already 30 minutes past your bedtime. You can do it tomorrow.

Sarah: (Whining) But, mommy, please, I'll just do half of what I wanted to do. Please, pleeeaaaase.

Me: (Reactively, in a loud and harsh voice): SARAH, STOP WHINING. I SAID NO. IT'S TIME TO GO TO SLEEP.

Then Sarah bursts into tears, all worked up because she is upset, explaining she is scared by my loud and harsh voice, which she calls the "strong voice." It takes time to calm her down so she can go to sleep, more time than it would have taken her to do the thing she wanted to do in the first place. Now I'm frustrated with her and angry with myself for escalating the situation.

With mindful action, I am proactive rather than reactive and the exchange goes something like this:

Me: No, you can't do that.

Sarah: Please, mommy, it will only take a few minutes.

Me: No, it is too late and I want you to get a good night's rest.

Sarah: Mommy, please, I really want to do it now.

Me: (Getting frustrated): Sarah, honey, it's already 30 minutes past your bedtime. You can do it tomorrow.

Sarah: (Whining): But, mommy, please, I'll just do half of what I wanted to do. Please, pleeeaaaase.

Me: (Taking a death breath and speaking in a softer voice): Sarah, honey, I said no and I told you why. Please stop asking. If you keep asking and whining, I am going to get frustrated and use my strong voice. You are going to cry and get upset, and we won't have an enjoyable bedtime. Let's skip all that and snuggle up and go to sleep.

Mindfulness Is a Little Vacation for Your Mind That Allows It to Relax and Rejuvenate

The key benefit is the ability to choose what you think about and do — in other words, the ability to act rather than react. A daily meditation practice, even as little as five minutes, can have these additional benefits.

1. *Reduce stress and anxiety.* Meditation calms the mind, which is the underlying premise for managing stress and anxiety. When we feel stressed and anxious, our minds are running at top speed in many different directions at the same time. Thus, the racing heart, tight muscles, and snappish reactions. Meditation and mindfulness can relax your mind and body to help you achieve a calmer state in which to face the world and all its challenges.

2. *Improve your ability to deal with difficult times and people.* Meditation and mindfulness are very helpful during difficult times, and when dealing with difficult people. Sometimes our reactions to events and people are only partly related to that event or person. Often some past experience is coloring our reaction, and perhaps making it more intense or problematic than the situation or person alone warrants. Meditation and mindfulness can help by calming your mind and helping you identify and understand the deeper questions that arise during these times.

3. *See yourself and your reality more clearly.* Meditation helps us connect to ourselves, at a deep level, so that we can better understand ourselves and why we do the things we do. Importantly, it also helps us see reality more clearly, which is the first step to making our lives better and less stressful.

4. *Increase focus and productivity.* Our lives with our many devices and distractions can make us feel frazzled and disrupt our ability to focus and pay attention. With all the obligations we handle in the numerous roles we play, meditation can restore our ability to focus and calm our mind so that we can manage all that we must.

5. *Allow you to let go of undesirable habits.* If you are trying, or want to try, to give up any habits that don't serve you well (for example, smoking, overeating, or a sugar addiction), meditation can help you achieve the clarity and calm needed to banish these habits.

6. *Increase compassion for yourself and others.* Meditation can increase our capacity for compassion toward ourselves and others. Compassion is an emotional response whereby one perceives another's problem and

genuinely wants to help resolve the problem. This is part of what humans do: People come to us with their problems, or to avoid future problems, and we help resolve or avoid the problems. Compassion is the foundation for good people skills. Without compassion, you cannot understand others, anticipate what they will do, or take preemptive steps to avoid problems. The compassionate person focuses on how others feel and is accepting of their perspective, whether or not she ultimately agrees with it.

7. *Improve communication skills.* Meditation can quiet our mind so that we can truly listen to others when they speak, rather than running our internal monologue and preparing what we'll say next. This improved ability to listen improves our communication skills since one of the most important aspects of communication is listening.

8. *Enhance creativity.* We need to be creative to find real solutions to life's problems. Each problem is unique, each person must be handled differently, and each solution carefully crafted. The best way to create unique solutions is to approach each situation with compassionate listening, which enables you to really understand the issues and what you and others need. That level of understanding can lead to long-lasting solutions that work for everyone.

9. *Develop perseverance.* Life requires perseverance. You must keep working, keep trying, and keep going. You must be able to walk away when things are not working, take a break, and come back fresh and ready. Meditation gives your brain the opportunity to rest and rejuvenate so that you can persevere.

How to Practice Mindfulness

I've been working on mindfulness for years. I'm still working on it. One cannot be mindful all the time. It takes practice and dedication. The concept is simple; the doing is difficult. There is no right or wrong way.

Be aware that the benefits of mindfulness and meditation happen after the meditation, not necessarily *during* the meditation. You may feel "I'm doing this wrong" or "This isn't working" or, even worse, "What's the point?" Keep trying. It gets easier and you will feel and see benefits. As with any new exercise plan, start easy and build the mindfulness muscle slowly. Following are ways to get started.

Be present. This is a great first step. Mindfulness means being present in the moment and focusing on what is happening right now. You can do this any-where, anytime. It is not zoning out, rather it is focusing in. I like to do this when I'm driving in the car by myself. Turn off the radio and drive in the quiet of your car. Look at the road. Notice the road signs. See the trees or buildings. Be present in the action and environment of driving. If other thoughts come into your mind to distract you, notice the thoughts and then let them go. If you find it helpful, mentally address the thought with a nod of your head or a quiet "Hello" and then let it go and again focus on the present moment of driving your car.

When something happens that leads to judgment (like another car pulling in front of you or driving too slowly), acknowledge that judgment, then let it go. Instead focus on what actually happened: "That car pulled in front of me." Period.

If you have a great idea that you want to remember, bookmark it in your brain to come back to it later. Right now, as you are being present, you are not work-ing on ideas or brainstorming. You are doing the opposite. You are giving your brain a break so that it can be refreshed and ready to work on ideas and handle life in a more thoughtful manner later.

Other ideas for where you can practice this kind of mindfulness are during your train or subway commute, while walking in your neighborhood or in the woods, or while sitting in a busy or quiet place. Throughout your day, notice times when you can take five minutes to focus on being present in the moment, and try it. You will have started your mindfulness practice and be on your way to acting deliberately and with intention.

There are additional ideas and exercises in the *Workbook* to help you practice being present on a daily basis.

Focus on breath. This too is something you can do almost anywhere, even in the midst of drama. Focus on your breath. Be deliberate in your breathing. While you practice being mindful in some of the ways described above, take long, slow, calming breaths, in and out. Some people prefer in through the mouth, out through the nose. I prefer in and out through the nose. Do whatever feels best for you. Slow your breath, breathe in deeply, hold it for a few seconds, and breathe out completely.

You can also sigh on the exhale. It is a great release of stress and negative energy. Imagine breathing in the "good" and releasing the "bad" on the exhale. It's simple, and it works. Deep breathing will relax the mind and body because you are giving your mind and body oxygen they need to feel good and work well, while releasing the waste carbon dioxide.

Take a few moments each day to breathe deeply, especially outdoors if you have a low-emissions outdoor space in which to sit or stroll. Follow the breathing exercises in the *Workbook* if you want more guidance.

Meditation

Meditation is the tool you will use for mindfulness. There are lots of theories about the practice of meditation and ways to meditate. My method is based on mindfulness meditation, which has its roots in Zen Buddhism. If you want to know more about mindfulness meditation and Zen Buddhism, check out the resources at the back of this book. For purposes of getting you started in your meditation practice, I'm simplifying things so you don't feel overwhelmed and can easily begin. As your practice grows, you can learn more about mindfulness meditation and more fully develop your practice in a way that works for you. Or, you can continue with the practice that you develop through this book. Choose what works best for you.

Where to meditate. Ideally, you want a quiet place where you can be alone and undisturbed for a period of time. Your bedroom. Your office with the door closed and phone and email notifications turned off. Your walk-in closet with the door closed. Even your car if you are having a day similar to many of my days.

I have a small Thai Buddha that I try to have in my place of meditation as a reminder of what I am trying to do. It's not necessary to have an object with you, but you could have any object that you find helpful. Maybe a photo of something you find peaceful, or a stone of some meaning, or Buddhist prayer beads, or rosary beads. Anything that marks the transition from living your life to focusing your mind and meditating.

How to sit. Ideally, you would sit on the floor, with legs crossed, on a small pillow so that your knees are lower than your hips. You can purchase a meditation pillow or cushion, or wooden meditation seat. Or you can sit on a regular pillow that feels comfortable. Having special items to mark the "event" of meditation can be helpful, but it's not necessary. If sitting on the floor doesn't work for you, you can sit in a chair.

The key is that your back should be straight, not leaning against anything. Your neck should be positioned so that your spine and neck are aligned. Your hands should be on your knees, or folded with palms up in your lap. With hands on your knees, you can rest your hands with palms down, or you can assume the meditation pose of palms up with thumb and index finger touching (in a position similar to "OK"). Generally, a palms-down pose is more calming, and a palms-up pose is more invigorating. I usually assume a palms-down pose because calming is almost always what I need.

Eyes open or closed. Either is fine. Some people find that closing their eyes is helpful because they do not become distracted by their surroundings. Others find that closing their eyes causes them to get lost in their thoughts rather than focusing their minds. I usually close my eyes, but some days I don't. Try it both ways and do whatever works for you.

Now let's meditate. Start by sitting comfortably and resting your hands in the position of your choice. Either close your eyes or soft focus on a spot on the floor about six feet in front of you. Focus on your breath. Take several deep breaths to calm your body and signify that you are beginning your meditation practice. Now sit quietly. Ideally, you won't move, not much, but if your nose itches or you become really uncomfortable, then you can move as you need to deal with those kinds of discomforts. Know that in traditional Buddhist meditation, you are not to move, at all, *no matter the discomfort.* The purpose is to learn to deal with discomforts without reaction, which translates to a calm handling of life's discomforts.

What's your goal? To not have a constant running commentary in your head. To not follow every thought that crosses your mind — in other words, to not follow every bone into the corner. You'll see this is easier said than done. By way of example, I'll share my typical thought patterns when I begin my meditation:

Thought: Running through my to-do list, making sure I didn't forget anything. Work things. Mom things. Every-things.

Calm response: Thank you. That is important. Once my mind is calm and clear, I will go over that list and plan my day.

Thought: Loads of great ideas.

Calm response: Thank you. Those are really great ideas. Let me note that thought to bookmark it for later, then when my mind is calm and clear, I will work with that thought to make a great plan or implement it right away.

Thought: Something random, like *my hands feel dry.*

Calm response: Yes *(or no, as is appropriate). Breathe. Focus on my breath.*

About five to seven minutes into my meditation, I finally start to feel a sense of calm and from there it is much easier and more enjoyable. I am able to regulate my thoughts, focus on what I choose, acknowledge thoughts that are not within my chosen focus, and let them pass. Usually, at some point I get lost in my thoughts again, so when I realize I am "chasing all the bones" of my thoughts, I remind myself to focus on what I choose and bring myself back to the meditation by focusing, again, on my breath. When I finish, I feel calm and ready to handle my busy life with clarity.

Release judgment. As you meditate, judgment is not allowed. Banish it. If you find it helpful, notice your thoughts in a way that will allow you to simply "report" them by writing them down. I don't actually write my thoughts down, but the exercise of approaching them as if I am going to helps me keep the nonjudgmental "reporter" attitude during my meditation. Don't judge the thoughts or yourself or your ability (or perceived inability) to get this meditation thing right. It's not about right and wrong, it's about what works for you.

What to do with all those thoughts. Some people suggest seeing your thoughts being placed on logs floating down a river, and just letting them float away. I like to put some of my thoughts — things that I want to address later — on a round floatie in the waterpark's lazy river so I know they will come back around to me again. Then I need not worry about the helpful thoughts or good ideas getting away from me forever.

USE MUSIC

Music has a tremendously relaxing effect on our minds and bodies, affecting our physiological functions, slowing the pulse and heart rate, lowering blood pressure, and decreasing the levels of stress hormones. Slow and quiet classical music is proven to provide these benefits, but every person has their own musical preferences, so find what works best for you. Listen during your commute or your yoga or meditation practice. You can also play relaxing music softly in the background in your office or home.

The Key Is Just Do It

The best way to develop a meditation practice is to start, then to keep trying every day. Some days, it feels like it will never work. Some days, it works easily. Approach it like a child, with an open mind, curiosity, a belief that you can do it, and with perseverance. If you have children, or have ever helped a child learn something difficult like riding a bike or reading, think back to the things you said and the advice you gave.

"It's difficult, but if you keep at it, you'll get it."

"Don't get discouraged, you are getting better every day, even if you don't feel like it yet."

"One day, it will just come to you if you keep trying."

"Everyone has trouble learning how to do this; it's hard. But everyone learns how to do it if they keep trying."

Be compassionate with yourself. In the 21st century, our brains are constantly inundated with information, making it very difficult to slow down. In addition, because we each have our own unique neurological profile for attention and stimulation, some will find meditating easier than others. In other words, don't beat yourself up if you find meditation difficult. It is.

In *Buddha's Brain: The Practical Neuroscience of Happiness, Love & Wisdom*, Rick Hanson, Ph.D., and Richard Mendius, M.D., provide useful tools to help you adapt your meditation practice to make it work for your brain. They suggest, among other tools, setting an intention so that your brain has a clear focus when meditating. Your intention could be "I will try" or "I am practicing" or "I am focusing on my breath." Set a simple intention so that you can be successful.

Another tool to quiet the running commentary in your brain is replacing that commentary with a mantra. I like "I have enough. I do enough. I am enough." Your mantra can be any word or phrase that has meaning for you, or it can be a simple word like "breathe." Try different mantras and find what works for you. You can try the mantras available in the *Workbook* and guided meditations available at my website, www.JamieSpannhake.com.

The key is to keep doing it. Every day. Without judgment. Even if you only have five minutes. Even if you feel like it's not working. Even if you feel like it's a waste of your time. And if you didn't meditate yesterday as planned, then start again today.

Yoga

Yoga is a great form of what's called moving meditation that can calm your mind and body. Yoga consists of body movements that include breath control, meditation, and the adoption of specific body postures, practiced for health and relaxation. Yoga coordinates your breath with your movements so that both your mind and body can relax. It also stretches and strengthens the muscles to provide a feeling of calm and wellness.

As part of your meditation practice, I encourage you to develop a weekly yoga practice. Ideally, I'd love to practice yoga an hour every day, but my life does not easily permit that, and I haven't been able to successfully incorporate it into my day in a way that works for me. So, once a week is my "attainable goal." (See below.)

If you are currently a yogi, you can practice at home or at a studio. I practice at home regularly, and at a few local studios when my schedule permits. There are many apps and online resources for classes. (See the selection at the back of this book.) If you are not a regular practitioner of yoga, I encourage you to attend an in-person class at a yoga studio (rather than a gym) prior to practicing at home so that the teacher can help you with alignment to ensure you do not injure yourself. An experienced yoga teacher can also show you modifications for postures that may be too difficult or inappropriate for your body and ability.

If you are not able to attend a yoga class in person, start with the movements called Sun Salutations at home. You can learn how to do these by searching for "sun salutation" on YouTube. This is a good, easy start to a beginner yoga practice and has many benefits.

ATTAINABLE GOALS: SUCCESS BREEDS SUCCESS

I mention that yoga once a week is my "attainable goal." When setting goals, it is important to be realistic, especially regarding the amount of time you have, as we discussed previously. This is particularly important to staying motivated because continued failures to achieve goals can leave us feeling demoralized. Be sure your goals are attainable by setting your goals in three parts: aspirational, realistic, and minimum. You need to really push yourself to reach an aspirational goal. You need to put in effort to achieve your realistic goal. And you can feel successful so long as you reach your minimum goal.

Mindful Inaction

It is important to note that not acting also has value. Sometimes when we are practicing mindfulness, what we learn is that our inaction can be very powerful. It is often valuable to sit with ideas, things, people, circumstances, problems, or life, and not act. As you practice mindfulness, consider both mindful action and mindful inaction. See the *Workbook* for daily practices of mindful inaction.

More Mindfulness

Retreats. If you have the ability to attend a meditation or yoga retreat, it is an amazing experience. It is the perfect way to re-center, regroup, and jump-start a better approach to life. I started this book and really focused my meditation practice with a yoga and meditation retreat with Cyndi Lee at Kripalu Center for Yoga & Health in Stockbridge, Massachusetts. Many retreats are surprisingly affordable, especially if you stay in minimalist accommodations like the dorm-style rooms at Kripalu. I prefer a retreat alone so that I can direct my own experience without being influenced by others and considering others' needs. But many people prefer doing a retreat with one or a few friends. I offer up this idea, though: If you don't usually like being alone, maybe that's exactly the reason to go on a retreat alone. You might learn something new about yourself or develop a new perspective. You are strong; you can handle it!

Zen Buddhism. If you want more mindfulness tools than meditation, yoga, and retreats, you can set about becoming a practitioner of Zen Buddhism. See the "Resources" section for more information about Zen Buddhism.

An Attitude of Gratitude

Many thought leaders, from Brené Brown to the Dalai Lama, tout the benefits of living with an attitude of gratitude. This is different than positive thinking in the face of real adversity. Rather, it is seeing life for the reality that it is, and being grateful for what's good about it even when some parts are not good. After your daily meditation, stop and think about the things for which you are grateful. I write mine in a "gratitude journal" several times each week.

Also try this in the face of adversity. My friend Diane Costigan, who is Director of Coaching at a large law firm in New York City, taught me this phrase when

I was working with her as a coach: *"What I like about it is ...."* This is a great way to live with an attitude of gratitude. It can also make you laugh in the face of trouble. For example, I lost my cellphone (disaster!), but what I like about it is ... I can get an early upgrade to a better phone. This is not always appropriate; some things just aren't likable in any way. But for many of our day-to-day annoyances and discomforts, this phrase can be magical.

Dealing With Anxiety

I suffer from anxiety. Clinical anxiety is a real thing. It includes generalized anxiety and panic disorders. It's not just getting easily annoyed or irritated or having a racing heart. It can cloud your mind and thought processes, inhibit your personality, and prevent you from enjoying your life, especially your social life. It is a true struggle.

I took medication for anxiety for nearly four years. I knew it was time for help beyond what I could manage on my own after a particularly stressful time at work. I was handling a large corporate arbitration that was extremely contentious. Opposing counsel was a dreadful person who flat-out lied to the arbitrator on numerous occasions. During one telephonic hearing with all counsel and the arbitrator, I was sitting in my office with the phone on speaker, listening to opposing counsel spout lies. I could feel my blood pressure rising, my heartbeat increasing, which at first felt normal for the situation. But then it went beyond normal. I began shaking. My mind began racing. I was having a hard time concentrating and breathing normally. I don't recall exactly how that hearing ended, but I remember getting out of my office and walking the entire city block twice before I began to feel a little more normal. But my heart rate didn't return to a normal resting rate.

From then on, my heart rate was at least 90 beats a minute, even when I was trying to go to sleep. When I did sleep, I had terrible dreams in which someone or something was after me and trying to kill me. I woke up in a near state of panic each morning and things only got worse as the day went on. I was shaking by the end of most days, unable to calm down or quiet my mind. I had been building up to this massive anxiety, just holding it at bay. Now it was released and I couldn't manage it anymore. I went to my doctor, who prescribed a selective serotonin reuptake inhibitor (SSRI). This worked really well for me, as did yoga and talk therapy with my wonderful therapist.

My point in telling you this is twofold. First, if you are taking medication for anxiety, do not stop your medication without discussing it with your doctor. Medication can be necessary for some people and some circumstances. It was necessary for me to "reset" my body and mind to get back to a place where I can manage my anxiety without it.

Second, whether you have clinical anxiety or situational anxiety or no anxiety, meditation and mindfulness are helpful. With a regular meditation practice and other tools, I am able to manage my anxiety without medication. For now. There may come a time when I am not able to live my best life because I find I can no longer manage the anxiety alone, even though I meditate and practice yoga regularly. If that time comes, I'll go back to medication without any shame.

For situational anxiety, meditation and mindfulness can solve the problem. Situational anxiety comes from worrying about what might happen in the future. Mark Twain had some apt words here: "I ... have known a great many troubles, but most of them never happened." Don't waste your time wringing your hands about things that might go wrong. Prepare, control what you can (which is often very little), and let the rest go. Don't be so attached to the outcome. Focus on the moment and the process, putting one foot in front of the other. Remember that no matter what happens, you will be able to handle it. Through mindfulness and meditation, you can begin approaching problems in this way, especially if you have created a reliable support network to assist when needed. (See the chapter "Ask for Help" to create your support network.)

Reality Check

Very few people are mindful all the time. Sometimes I'm not mindful. Sometimes I lose my patience. Sometimes I snap at my daughter and colleagues. Sometimes my reactions are "mindless." This often happens when I'm overcommitted or I have a great plan but something completely unanticipated screws the whole thing up, like a child getting sick or a snow day at school. You will have moments like this. In these moments, take a deep breath, give yourself a break, commit to keep trying to be mindful, and move on.

Focusing on your "failure" doesn't help and further distracts you from getting back to a place of mindfulness. You're not perfect. I'm not perfect. Nobody is perfect. Just try.

TOOLS FOR HANDLING ANXIETY

You can combat anxiety by increasing the levels of serotonin in the brain. Serotonin is a neurotransmitter, a kind of chemical messenger that helps the brain function. More specifically, serotonin is a "feel good" neurotransmitter and a mood stabilizer that boosts feelings of wellness and balance. When serotonin levels are optimal, you are able to think more clearly, act rather than react, and address stressful situations with calm and clarity. There are ways to naturally increase serotonin levels in the brain.

- **Eat a healthy diet.** A healthy, balanced diet is important for optimal serotonin levels. In particular, fish, eggs, nuts and seeds, pineapples, and complex carbohydrates (like fresh fruits and vegetables and whole grains) increase serotonin levels. It is also important to limit added sugars because sugar disrupts normal chemical reactions in the brain, which can inhibit serotonin processing and production. Supplement your healthy diet with B vitamins, fish oil, holy basil, rodiola, and L-tyrosine, all of which help the brain produce more serotonin.

- **Exercise.** It is the most effective way to increase serotonin levels. There are no side effects, and it always works. As little as 30 minutes of brisk walking three times each week will help.

- **Get body work.** Methods including massage, acupuncture, acupressure, and reflexology relieve stress and boost serotonin levels.

- **Grab sunlight.** Many people suffer from seasonal affective disorder (SAD) in the winter months when there is much less sunlight. This is because the brain has less serotonin when there is less sunlight. Spend at least 15 minutes each day in the sun. Go for a walk before work or after lunch, or sit by a sunny window on the commuter train. You can also purchase a light box for your office or home.

- **Use your mind.** Thinking about past happy experiences, or looking at photos of those experiences, can boost serotonin levels. The same is true for keeping a gratitude journal and daydreaming about happy times. Spending time with loved ones and talk therapy with a trusted therapist are also great ways to get out of your head and allow serotonin in.

- **Take two days for your mental health.** Use the first day to catch up on stuff. Don't let your colleagues know you are working, so you can handle existing tasks without new tasks being added. Use the second day as a day off to boost your serotonin levels by finding some peace and mental clarity.

"Choose Which Thoughts to Follow" Review

1. Remember to be the lion and choose which thoughts to follow.

2. Practice mindfulness every day by being present in the moment and breathing deeply, especially in the face of difficult circumstances and people.

3. Start or continue developing a daily meditation practice, for as little as five minutes each day.

4. Try a yoga practice. Or if you have a yoga practice, continue it on a regular basis.

5. Develop an attitude of gratitude, appreciating the good things even when times are rough. Incorporate *"What I like about it is ..."* into your daily language.

6. Try to be mindful. When you "fail," move on and just keep trying. Nobody is perfect.

PART 2

ACT

We become what we repeatedly do.
— Stephen Covey

ASK FOR HELP

You like to be independent,
but you will need to learn to ask for help.
It doesn't make you weak.
– Taya Kyle

Giving feels fantastic
and for there to be a Giver,
there must be a Receiver,
so allowing yourself to receive is an act of love.
– Rebecca O'Dwyer

We must acknowledge that asking for help is not only acceptable, it is smart, strong, and wise. We may be able to do it all ourselves, but that doesn't mean that we should.

If you, like me, do not naturally seek help from others, this will be a learning process for you. I can do a lot, all at the same time. And there is a part of me that celebrates myself when I think about *all the things* that I can handle. I even like the idea that other people are looking at me and enviously saying, "I don't know how you do it all!"

But there is a price to pay.

Mental overload, emotional drain, extreme calendaring and planning, and ultimately exhaustion. Nobody can keep up a break-neck pace indefinitely. And what happens when something throws a monkey wrench in your carefully crafted plan? A simple school delay for snow might be the final straw, the one thing that makes the entire system come crashing down. And then what? You can melt into a puddle, or you can ask for help. Maybe even more important, by allowing others to help you, you can "find" more time.

Create Your Support Network

To get the help you need to live the life you want, invest in creating a support network. A support network is a group of people who support one another and make room for every member of the network. For some people, this can be family members; for others, it can be friends; and for others, it could be paid support, like a nanny, housekeeper, or personal assistant.

Think about all the people in your life who are geographically close to you, and list them out in your journal or the *Workbook*. These are the potential members of your support network.

- Family
- Friends
- Neighbors
- School teachers and staff
- Others

Get the Help You Need

Now look back at your details from the first chapter where you defined your framework for what you want in your life, and make a list of all the tasks that you could allow someone else to handle. Then consider "The Three B's" exercise from Part 1. Are there responsibilities that you don't personally need to do, in other words, responsibilities that you can "barter"? Can anyone in your support network handle one or more of those responsibilities? For example, would it make life easier if you and another parent took turns each week driving your and her kids to school or after-school activities? If a dog walker took your dogs on a hike once a week? If you could rely on a neighbor to get your kids off the school bus when you are running late?

Go through every detail for which you could use help and consider if someone in your support network can assist. Start with non-paid sources. If after going through all the non-paid sources in your support network, you still have obligations that you'd like to "barter," start thinking about people to pay or paid services that could handle these obligations.

For my support network, I have a group of friends whose kids attend school with my daughter that I can call upon last minute if I am running late for school pickup. I also keep a list of babysitters posted in my kitchen in case I want a night out or have a late meeting. And I have two last-minute contacts for mid-day dog walks in case I get stuck at the office and can't get home to let them out myself. I also have a house cleaning service that comes every other week; I can keep things tidy in between, but the real cleaning happens twice a month.

I also use several paid online services. I like to have new clothes about once a quarter, but I don't like to shop and I don't like to spend my time shopping. So I use Stitch Fix, where a stylist shops for me and sends me five items every three months. It's awesome. I also shop online for most items, from holiday gifts to groceries, which are then delivered to my house or straight to the gift recipient.

I use Chewy.com for all my pet needs, and set an automatic delivery and payment schedule for dog and cat food and supplies, including my elderly dogs' medication. There are other similar services for many things that you need: groceries, clothing, household items, pet supplies, prescriptions, gifts, handmade treasures, and so on. See the "Resources" section for more ideas.

If you can't barter it — either because you need to handle the responsibility yourself, or you don't have anyone in your support network to handle it for you — then focus on "bettering it" or "bagging it," as discussed in Part 1. As a reminder, you can "better" an obligation by doing it in a way that makes it more enjoyable for you; or you can "bag" an obligation by deciding that it's not necessary at all.

Re-evaluate

After you have bartered, bettered, or bagged some of your obligations, rework the time commitment necessary for your framework for the life you want that you created in Part 1. There's a guided exercise for this in the *Workbook*. You may find that you can have more without doing more since you now have a support network to help you. The point is to ensure that your expectations are realistic so that you have not set yourself up to fail.

Raise Your Expectations

It may seem counterintuitive to raise your expectations when we are discussing delegating and trusting others to handle things that you would normally handle yourself. But you can raise your expectations regarding what responsibilities others could handle. My friend Tal Fagin tells of the morning she was rushing around the kitchen to fix breakfast and lunches for her three kids before school. In the midst of this, she looked up and saw her 11-year-old daughter sitting at the breakfast counter waiting for her bowl of cereal. It suddenly occurred to her that an 11-year-old can pour her own bowl of cereal! This was not something that she, as the mother, had to do.

This made me realize that I could do this, too. For example, my eight-year-old daughter can handle packing her lunchbox for school if I keep healthy choices readily available that are easy to prepare. I don't do this every day, but it's comforting to know I can rely on someone else to prepare lunch, if necessary, on a morning when I have too many other responsibilities.

Raise your expectations for your spouse, kids, close friends, and hired helpers. Walking the dog, fixing meals, doing laundry, picking the kids up from school — others can do these things. When allowing your children to handle responsibilities, you could opt to pay them an allowance, or you could focus on the personal responsibility aspect. Either is fine.

Support Someone Else

Remember that being a member of a support network means that you support others, too. Don't just be a taker; also give. This has often caused me to hesitate. I know I will be expected to participate, and I do not have the extra time. But remember that giving does not necessarily mean giving of your time. There are many ways to give: words of thanks and kindness; small tokens of appreciation, like a handwritten thank-you note or small gift card to a local coffee shop; just being a friend and talking together; or payment if a member of your network is someone you hire like a nanny, housekeeper, dog walker, or driver.

Reality Check

There is one important mindset that you must embrace to utilize the resources in your support network: You must dispense with a "my way or the highway" attitude. When you ask others to handle things for you, you must accept that they will not handle them exactly the way you would. And, as much as we all believe our way is the best — or only — way, that's usually not true. Let others try it their way before you decide that their way will not work for you.

Delegating can be difficult because it inherently means giving up some control over the process. This is one of my challenges. But I try to remember the unexpected beauty that can appear when I loosen my grip on control. One of the first ways I experienced the positive effects of less control was with watercolor paints. When I paint with watercolors, I have much less control over the outcome than with other paints like acrylics. Watercolors are, of course, mixed with water and when I place the paint on the paper, the water in it flows in ways that are not necessarily at my direction. Rather, there's always at least a small surprise in the result. The lack of control that makes me uncomfortable is precisely what makes the painting beautiful.

As you utilize your support network and delegate tasks, be careful that you are actually delegating and releasing your tight grip on control. Otherwise, you are merely creating additional management responsibilities for yourself. Be honest: If you micromanage the people to whom you delegate, you aren't saving yourself any time and you are frustrating them. To delegate effectively, you must use your energy to find a competent and cooperative helper, be very clear in your directions and expectations, and let him or her take the responsibility. There may be growing pains, both in your ability to give effective directions and your helper's ability to deliver as expected, but it will be worth it.

"Ask for Help" Review

1. Identify all the people who could be a part of your support network.

2. Consider all the areas where you could use support, including the detailed items that someone in your support network could handle.

3. Consider services that you can set up to automatically handle some of your obligations.

4. Re-evaluate the time needed for the framework of the life you desire, as you previously explored in Part 1.

5. Expect others — especially those in your family — to actively participate as members of your support network.

6. Delegate effectively. Find the right people, be clear, and let them handle it.

GET ORGANIZED

For every minute spent organizing,
an hour is earned.
– Anonymous

Organizing is what you do before you
do something so that when you do it,
it is not all mixed up.
– A.A. Milne

We've discussed how to create space in your mind through mindfulness and meditation so that you can handle life without feeling overwhelmed. In this chapter, we will learn how to create this same kind of calm in your physical environment and your daily schedule by getting organized. When you are organized, you don't waste time and energy trying to find whatever you need to be successful. Rather, your resources are readily available to you, which decreases anxiety, increases focus, and reduces overwhelm.

Organize Your Space

There are many great books on organizing, but if you want to stay organized so that you are prepared and efficient, there is one initial step that all organizers know is crucial to continued success: having less "stuff."

My favorite resource for pruning your belongings is the popular book *The Life-Changing Magic of Tidying Up* by Marie Kondo. I read the book and followed her advice: Get rid of things that do not "spark joy." To paraphrase Kondo's advice, items that do not bring you joy have no place in your life. For example, if you are keeping a gift that your favorite aunt gave you simply because you "should," even though you don't like the item, it may be causing you grief. How? Every time you look at it, you feel badly because you never use it, or maybe worse, you don't like it. This makes you feel ungrateful, which makes you not like yourself. That gift would be better utilized if you gave it to someone who would like it or donated it to someone who could use it. Not having the gift in your space would help you avoid the negative feelings that seeing it causes you. Get rid of it.

Another example is clothes that are two sizes too small. If every time you look at those clothes, you feel fat because you can't fit into them, then they are stealing your joy. Get rid of them. When you get to that size again, you can reward yourself by buying new clothes. That is more incentive than wearing your old clothes anyway!

As Kondo says, occasionally you will get rid of something that you wish you had kept, but a vast majority of the time, you won't miss those items at all. Follow her advice and pare down your belongings all at once to open up your space and change your life. Then you can organize the items you enjoy, need, and use.

How to Reduce Your Stuff

Moving things out of your space can be difficult. Kondo recommends working in categories of items rather than by room. This is sound advice. For example, you may not realize that you have multiples of the same item if they are stored in different locations throughout your space. Start by determining the categories of your items, such as clothing, books, papers, toys, kitchen/cooking items, tools and hardware, miscellaneous items, and sentimental items. There is a helpful list in the *Workbook* if you need more guidance. Kondo recommends starting with clothing and ending with sentimental items.

Choose your first category, which could be any category but sentimental items since those are often the most difficult to assess. Gather all the items from that category in one space, if possible. Before you start assessing your items, Kondo recommends that you start with a mindful practice of thanking your space for being a good physical space for you. Think of all the good times that have occurred in your space or all the love that fills the space, and be grateful that you have your physical space. Then go through each item and determine whether it "sparks joy" in you, per Kondo's method. There is no magic to "sparking joy." It means whatever it means to you. If this phrase doesn't resonate with you yet, I highly recommend Kondo's book.

For me, the questions I suggest asking yourself when assessing each item are:

- Do you like it? Why?

- Do you want it? Why?

- Do you use it? When was the last time you used it?

- Do you need it? For what and when?

Know that even if you answer "no" to each of those questions, if the item "sparks joy" for you, that is reason enough to keep it. But be honest with yourself. You are reducing the amount of your "stuff" for yourself in order to calm your physical and mental space. No one is forcing you to get rid of things you truly want to keep. You want items that benefit your well-being, not things that negatively affect you.

The final mindful action to take when reducing your clutter, according to Kondo, is to thank each item that you determine to move out of your space. This may feel awkward at first, but the more you do it, the easier it will become. This small step provides the closure that we need when we "lose" something. This "thank you" allows us to avoid any feelings of guilt for getting rid of an item that, at one time, meant something to us.

With your thanks, put the item in a bag or box and move it out of your physical space, either to donate or throw away. If you are donating, know in advance where you will take the items and take them as soon as a bag or box is full.

Rules for an Organized Space

1. *Find a place for everything, and always put things away.* I have a place for everything, and lots of those places are labeled so other family members can follow my lead by putting things in their place (which they sometimes do). This way, I know where everything is — or needs to go. By Friday afternoon, my kitchen island counter is often filled with items that made their way into the house during the week but were never put away. So sometime between Friday evening and Sunday afternoon, I spend 20 to 30 minutes going through that stuff and tossing it out or putting it away. Clutter never lasts more than one week in our house, so it never gets so out of hand that it's a big project or huge time-suck to tidy up and stay organized.

2. *Keep the clutter out of your house and office.* Clutter can make you feel anxious. A cluttered home or office makes me so anxious that I forget something I need every time I leave! In her wildly popular Netflix show *Tidying Up*, Kondo explores this concept in depth, giving real-life examples of how clutter negatively affects people emotionally, relationally, and spiritually. But what if you love freebies like I do? Ask yourself if you really need another T-shirt that you'll never wear, another plastic water bottle, or a key chain? Probably not. It will take up space that you could be using for items that you actually need and use.

3. *Identify problem areas and make a plan.* Do dishes pile up in the sink too often? Does it seem that the mail is lying on the dining room table all the time? Must you search for your keys every time you leave the house? Identify problem areas and brainstorm solutions by first assessing why the problem exists. For example, perhaps the mail is always lying on the table because it sits close to the entrance to your house and there's no other handy place to put the mail where you'll remember to deal with it later. Maybe all you need is a mail bin hanging on the wall in the kitchen, or next to the door. Drop the mail there each day and plan to go through it once a week.

   As for keys, maybe all you need is a little hook by the door. Hang your keys there every time you come in, and they will always be there.

   For the dishes, maybe you could set aside five minutes each morning to load or unload the dishwasher or wash dishes. I like to start my coffee brewing in the morning and deal with the dishes while I wait for it to finish. The sink may be full of dirty dishes when I go to bed, but by the time I'm drinking my coffee each morning, it's cleaned up.

4. *Do a little every day.* The key to staying organized is doing a little every day to keep things in order. When you don't let things get completely out of order, the reset to organization is quick and easy, and thus easier to maintain.

Organize Your Time

One of the best ways to keep all your various responsibilities in order and successfully handled is to organize your time. Organize your day so that you use your time as efficiently as possible.

Part of organizing your time is planning. When I am overwhelmed with work and life, I want to jump in as quickly as possible and tackle things. Who has time to plan? Resist that temptation. Take a breath, and take the time to plan. Would you build a house without first drafting a plan? Of course not. Take the same approach to your day and your life. You actually save time when you make a good and thoughtful plan. And when you take five minutes to meditate *before* you plan, your planning will go more smoothly and efficiently. Meditation will clear your mind of the noise and allow you to breathe, slow down, and think. If you need help with meditation, review the information in the chapter "Choose Which Thoughts to Follow" in Part 1.

How to Approach Your Time

1. *Plan everything and put it on the calendar.* Plan on a yearly, weekly, daily, and by project basis. Keep one calendar with everything on it — work deadlines and appointments, family obligations, and personal items (like exercise) — and sync it to all your devices.

   My friend Vanessa Price, who is a solo attorney in Southaven, Mississippi, works about 50 hours a week. She is married to a lawyer and has two school-age children. For her, the only way she can manage work, life, and family is by sitting down every Sunday with her husband and kids to plan the week. "We lay out all items on the calendar: kids' activities, soccer, baseball games, driving the kids, gym classes, work stuff, everything," she says.

   Like my friend, I put everything in my Google calendar, which I can access on all my devices (work laptop and phone, personal laptop and phone, and any other device with internet). I follow the calendar. This is especially important for me when it comes to exercising. I can always find a reason not to work out, but if I have my workout scheduled in the calendar, including the distance I plan to run or the time that my tennis clinic starts, then I'm much less likely to blow it off.

   When things don't go as planned, I recalibrate and review at the end of each day. Of course, no matter how carefully we plan our lives, we don't have control over everything. Your calendar is your aspirational plan — the way you want the day to go if you could control everything. But not everything will go as planned, so remain flexible and readjust when things change.

As you organize your responsibilities and activities on your calendar, consider and include, if possible, the people in your support network who can help you. My ex-husband and I have a successful co-parenting relationship for our daughter in large part because we have a shared family calendar on Google. We may not be married, but we still need to operate as a family for the benefit of our daughter. Bring support people into your organizing, set up a shared calendar, and decrease the time needed to coordinate, remind, and follow up. You can even send a calendar invite to your support people, just in case they don't review the calendar as often as needed.

2. *"Chunk" your work into manageable timeframes and take breaks.* It's easier to keep your time organized and your efforts focused in smaller chunks of time, so schedule your work in 45- to 90-minute increments. Then take a break or switch to something else. If you must keep working, switch to a separate project or to a new task within the same project, for example, switching from writing to reviewing documents or responding to client email. If you can, schedule in short breaks — go for a walk, do five minutes of stretching, or engage in a meditation mini-session. Also schedule in a longer break each day, if possible, where you can get some exercise for rejuvenation and return to work with increased focus.

3. *Use your time creatively and multitask wisely.* Schedule snippets of "extra" time. Early on a weekend morning before the family wakes up, or in the evening after everyone else goes to bed, can provide more time for work or personal tasks. If you have more control over your schedule, you can work hours that fit your life — for example, not working after the kids get home from school until after they go to bed, then heading back to the office, or into your home office, for late evening hours.

Also get creative with multitasking. Despite research on the negative impact of multitasking on productivity, you can multitask wisely by combining an intellectual task with a mindless task. Some examples? Dictate a blog post or presentation or email response on your smartphone while walking to work, then convert it to text and email it to yourself. Or dictate a to-do list and client updates into a small digital recorder while driving between meetings or events.

"Get Organized" Review

1. Reduce your "stuff."

2. Eliminate the clutter.

3. Find a place for everything, and put it in its place every time.

4. Keep ahead of the disarray by not bringing unnecessary "stuff" into your space.

5. Effectively plan your time and activities in your calendar.

6. Share your calendar with your support network.

7. Follow the calendar, recalibrate when things change, and review at the end of each day.

PART 3

THINK

Your beliefs become your thoughts,
Your thoughts become your words,
Your words become your actions,
Your actions become your habits,
Your habits become your values,
Your values become your destiny.
– Mahatma Gandhi

ENOUGH TIME

Time is a created thing.
To say "I don't have time" is to say
"I don't want to."
– Lao Tzu

To achieve great things, two things are needed:
a plan, and not quite enough time.
– Leonard Bernstein

One of the realities in life is time. Time is what it is. You can't "make" time. Knowing that, we often get caught up in the belief that we "just don't have enough time!" But it's not true. I know what you are saying: "Oh, yeah, it is true; I actually do not have time to do everything." I feel that way, too. Many nights I go to bed thinking about all the things I didn't do. Sometimes something bad happens as a result: I don't return a phone call quickly enough and lose the opportunity to help a new client, or I don't iron the patches on my daughter's Girl Scout uniform so she's the only Daisy without flower petals on her vest. I hear you.

But the problem with time is not that we do not have enough of it; the problem is that we are trying to do *everything*. Sure, more time would be nice, but that's not what we really need. What we need is to transform our relationship with time by narrowing our definition of what we must do. By working through the book so far, you have more narrowly defined what you *must* do, how best to handle those obligations mindfully, and who can help you. You can transform your relationship with time further by reframing the way you think about time and using language that helps you express that thinking.

Even if you aren't convinced that you actually have enough time, I encourage you to experiment with the ideas in this chapter. Even if you think I am wrong, and you are convinced that you need more time, this chapter will help you.

By changing the way you think about time, and the way you talk to yourself about time, you can transform your relationship with it.

Try the exercises in this chapter. The investment of your time and energy is small; the return can be enormous.

Reality of Time

The reality of time is that we have quite a bit of it. Each week has 168 hours. ONE HUNDRED SIXTY-EIGHT. That's a lot of hours! Assume you sleep 56 hours a week (because that is really what you need) and work 40 hours each week. That still leaves you 72 hours each week in which to handle everything else! That's almost like two additional full-time jobs' worth of time for your other priorities. Even if you work 60 hours each week, that still leaves you 52 hours, which is more than another full-time job.

Even when we know this, it still *feels* like there isn't enough time. Part of the problem is how we think about time. Our Western culture thinks of time as linear. This means time that has passed is gone forever, and wasted if not used effectively. This conception keeps us running forward to make sure we use our time wisely, but there is another way to think about time. Some other cultures think of time as being circular: Time comes and goes. If time has passed, it isn't gone forever; it will come back around. Open your mind to changing the way you think about time.

Another part of the problem is how we *talk* about time. Many people would say this is semantics, but I disagree. I am a lawyer, so there are no "semantics." Words have meaning, and each word means something different than another, even if only slightly. That's why we have so many words in the English language. The words we use can be chosen to help or hinder us, used to say exactly what we mean, or sort of what we mean. So stop saying "I don't have enough time" or "I'm just so busy." Those words don't help you.

Think about other areas in your life where the words you use can affect an outcome. There's a guided exercise in the *Workbook* to help you. For example, if you continually tell yourself you are fat, it can make you feel depressed. Feeling depressed can lead to lack of motivation. Lack of motivation prevents you from exercising, which makes you feel more depressed. So you comfort yourself with chocolate ice cream, which makes the problem worse. The point is, whether you are truly overweight is less important than how you think about your weight. Even if it is true that you have more body fat than you desire, by changing the words you use, you can change the outcome. The words you use define who you are and what you do.

When I stopped saying "I don't have enough time," my life totally changed. I lost the feeling of constantly having to run from one activity to another. Maybe I am still running from one thing to another, but I don't feel the negative effects of it.

Change "I don't have enough time" to "I choose not to do that" or "I don't want to do that." Those phrases are different. Sometimes we want to do something, but, in light of our values and priorities, we choose not to. Other times, we just don't want to do it.

Why say "I choose not to do that" or "I don't want to do that"? Because it is true. Most things that we don't do are things we don't deem important enough to move from the bottom of our to-do list or things we don't *want* to do. In other words, they aren't directly within our values and priorities. As I've mentioned, I don't clean my house often enough. Why? Because I don't have time? No, because I don't want to and because a clean house has very little bearing on my effectiveness or happiness. I like a clean house, but I don't want to spend my time cleaning it. Similarly, I don't exercise every day. Why? Because, though I say I want to, if I am honest, I don't really want to. Admitting this takes honesty.

Learn to Say No to Others

After you are able to speak honestly with yourself, you can start speaking honestly to others when they ask you to take on responsibilities. It can be difficult to say no to other people and it seems easier when we say no followed by the excuse that we don't have time. Instead, try honesty. Say "No," period. If you feel you need to explain (though you probably don't), you can say "No" along with "but thank you for the opportunity" or "thank you for asking me" or "I don't want to do that" or "I choose not to do that." Most people will respect you for your honesty. By saying no this way, you will avoid the resentment of doing things that you don't want to do, a feeling often directed at yourself for saying yes when you really wanted to say no. If saying no in this way makes you uncomfortable, or if the other person does not respect your honesty, then simply say no. Period.

If you have a hard time saying no, you need practice to learn how to do it without feeling guilty (and you do not need to feel guilty). It may be hard in the

GOOD SLEEP IS THE FOUNDATION OF HEALTH

The quantity of your time asleep affects the quality of your time awake. Over a third of our life should be spent sleeping. This can feel like a waste of time, but it's not. Sleep-deprived people cannot function at their highest ability. Sleep deprivation decreases your ability to remember and process information. A good night's sleep can give us up to a threefold advantage in complex problem-solving. Also, cutting your sleep short by even an hour or two reduces the effectiveness of your immune system by about 25 percent, leading to more illness and disease. And did you know that lack of sleep increases the release of one of the hunger hormones that causes cravings for carbohydrates and sugars, making it much more difficult to maintain a healthy weight?

To stay healthy, you must give your body time to recover and refresh. Sleep provides this opportunity. The average adult requires seven to eight hours of sleep each night. Set a regular sleep schedule and stick to it, not altering your regular bedtime or awake time by more than one hour.

---

beginning, but focus on what's important to you and say yes to those things. Realize that saying yes to one thing often means saying no to something else. Don't say yes to others' priorities to the detriment of your own.

Act on Your Time Transformation

With your transformed relationship to time, focus on using your time for your priorities and values — the framework for your life that you created in Part 1. Make sure you have more things you want to do, fewer things you don't want to do, and more tools for handling those things. There's an exercise in the *Workbook* if you need ideas and guidance.

Here's an example of how.

Exercise is one area I have difficulty maintaining. Why? Because there are all kinds of exercise that I do not enjoy. I have tried to like group exercise classes, home workout DVDs, and trips to the gym. But I don't. Because I don't like them, I don't want to do them and don't use my time doing them. I need to find ways to be fit that I enjoy. The real question is: "What kind of exercise do I enjoy?"

Hiking with my dogs in the woods. Long walks. Yoga. Lifting weights. Tennis and running. I look forward to these activities so I will do them happily. I can "find" time to play tennis and run, even when I can't — or won't — fit a trip to the gym into my schedule.

Ask yourself, "What are the things I feel like I don't have time to do?" Then be honest with yourself and ask, "Do I really want to do those things?" If the answer is no, acknowledge it and accept it. Then apply the "Three B's" we discussed in Part 1.

- If you can "Bag It," that's great. Problem solved.

- If it really must be done, then "Barter It" and find someone else to do it.

- If someone else can't do it, then work on "Bettering It."

Start by considering what you are trying to achieve — in other words, why you must do it. If you can find a different way to achieve that goal, a way that you would enjoy, you are much more likely to get it done. I did this with running.

For years I tried to incorporate running into my life, but I hated it. I didn't want to bag it because I wanted a regular and effective cardiovascular work-out. I couldn't barter it because only I can get myself fit. Finally, about a year ago, I found a way to better it: I joined a running club with other women and a running coach. My membership came with a personalized running program designed by an experienced coach and a group of women who serve as my accountability partners. In the beginning, I could only run about a half-mile. After over a year, I've come to really like it and find time to run three to four times each week. I've raced a 5k nearly every month and even a five-mile race, with my times improving continually.

As you are figuring out ways to act on your transformed relationship with time, also consider altering your goals to better suit your current life. Keeping in mind the reality of time, as well as your values and priorities, you may need or want to change some of your goals. For example, if your goal is to go to the gym five days a week but you have a newborn baby who doesn't sleep through the night and you are up every two hours, you would benefit from altering your goal. Perhaps a more realistic goal that honors your current life would be one day each week at the gym plus four days of leisurely walks with your baby. Or maybe the fourth quarter of every year is the busiest time at work. This might

TO BETTER IT, CONSIDER WHAT YOU WANT TO ACHIEVE

When trying to better a task or goal, reflect on the reasons you must do the task or the reasons you set the goal in the first place. Was it to have more energy, earn more money, be a kinder person, improve a relationship? Sit quietly and focus on how achieving this goal will make you feel. Happy? Proud? Energized? Loved? Shift your focus to how great achieving it will make you feel, rather than the amount of time or energy you will need to achieve it. While it is important to stay positive, some people (like me) are also motivated by the possible negative outcome of not achieving a goal. If you find it helpful, consider what life will be like and how you will feel if you do not reach your goal. Write your answers in your journal or the *Workbook*.

---

not be the best time to pursue big goals for business development or train for a half-marathon. As your circumstances change, you can alter your goals to better fit those changes.

I do this with many things. I would like to run a half-marathon, but my priorities and schedule make monthly 5k races more suited to my current life. I would like to improve my tennis game at the same rate as some of my tennis partners, but they are retired from work and their kids are adults. They play three to four times each week, but I play only once or twice a week. I can't compare my progress to theirs; I can only compare it to my own. I could say that I can't do these things because I don't have time, but it's because they are not high enough on my priority list. If these goals for running and tennis were higher on my priority list, I would achieve them. But they aren't – at least not right now. Right now, I have not chosen to make them more important so they do not warrant more time. Maybe later they will.

Of course, shifting priorities around to achieve goals is possible. My friend Diane Costigan, who is a career coach among other things, is a great example of someone who shifted her priorities to achieve a long-time goal: She wanted to become a black belt in karate. She saved money, developed a consulting and coaching role for herself so she could tailor her schedule, then quit her job to train daily for hours. By the end of a year, she earned her black belt (and met the man she would eventually marry; he also was earning his black belt that year). She re-entered the workforce after that year and continued to build and improve her career, more invigorated and focused than before.

A Caveat About Obligations

Not all of life is enjoyable. When faced with lackluster obligations, analyze your attitude toward them. If you change your perspective, you may not need to change the responsibility. Shift your perspective to see life in a way that is better for you. As Henry David Thoreau said, "It's not what you look at that matters; it's what you see."

Shifting your perspective can make your life more enjoyable, allow you to focus on the good, and bring you to new creative solutions. We can shift our perspective by thinking or doing something differently to change ourselves, our situation, or others.

One simple way to shift your perspective is to change the words with which you describe your obligations: Think "I get to" instead of "I have to." For example, I don't enjoy cooking, but I "have" to cook many nights. Sure, sometimes we go out for dinner or eat leftovers, but every evening, someone has to cook food for us to eat, and many nights that someone is me. I can say, "Tonight I get to cook dinner for my family." It doesn't change the task, but it makes me think about how I get to choose what we eat; I get to ensure that our food is healthy; I get to talk to my daughter while we are in the kitchen together; and so on. It makes the obligation feel more like a choice.

Another way to shift your perspective is to change something in your environment. It could be something small, and it need not be related to the task you don't like. For example, maybe you dread attending weekly meetings every Monday. When Monday rolls around, drive a different route to work or try a new restaurant for lunch. The change isn't related to the problem, but by doing something differently, your mind can open to other possibilities. Eventually, you can move on to changing bigger things that have a more direct impact on the problematic issue.

Once you can look forward to doing things, you may find that the time to do them magically appears.

"Enough Time" Review

1. Stop saying you don't have enough time. Instead, say "I choose not to do that" or "I don't want to do that."

2. Use words and thoughts that help rather than hinder you.

3. Say no to responsibilities that are not within or in line with your values and priorities.

4. Apply the "Three B's" to tasks and responsibilities.

5. Shift your perspective to better handle lackluster responsibilities.

6. Think "I get to" rather than "I have to."

"SHOULD" NO MORE

Change the changeable, accept the unchangeable,
and remove yourself from the unacceptable.
– Denis Waitley

When you become a lover of what is,
the war is over.
– Byron Katie

Sometimes reality is not what you want it to be. You think things should be different, but they aren't. When you think things *should* be different than they are, you are arguing with reality. To paraphrase Byron Katie, founder of The Work and author of *Loving What Is*, when you argue with reality, you always lose.

Repeatedly losing that argument makes us unhappy. We are most unhappy when we argue with the reality of dealing with other people:

■ Your mother-in-law shouldn't correct the way you parent your children.

■ Your uncle shouldn't drink so much and be so loud.

■ Your colleagues shouldn't gossip so much.

■ Your nephew shouldn't sit at the dinner table with headphones on.

■ Your husband shouldn't leave his shoes in the middle of the living room.

■ Your children shouldn't ignore you.

But the truth is, they do.

Find Your Remedy for "Should"

Banish the "shoulds" from your life. Embrace reality. Embrace what is, especially when you cannot control the circumstance, process, or outcome.

The best way to handle difficult realities — the way things *should* be but aren't — is to accept that they exist and work with that knowledge. You can work with the difficult reality to find a remedy if you can control the circumstance, process, or outcome. For example, if your uncle drinks too much and embarrasses the family each time you go out to dinner, you can work with that knowledge to change the circumstance by choosing a restaurant that doesn't serve alcohol. Rather than repeatedly being annoyed or angry that your uncle drinks too much, you embrace the reality that he will continue to do so and change a circumstance that changes the outcome.

If you can't control the circumstance, process, or outcome, then the remedy is to change something in yourself or your life so you don't remain in that difficult reality. For example, when your nephew sits at the holiday dinner table wearing headphones and refusing to engage in conversation each year, you normally become frustrated and angry, in part because he is ignoring you. Next time, embrace the fact that he will be wearing headphones and ignoring you. You will arrive with no expectation of conversing with your nephew. Because you will not even try to engage him in conversation, your frustration will be lessened. By doing this, you have changed something within yourself that, in turn, changes the outcome. Another alternative is to decline the invitation to the holiday dinner because you know what will happen there. With this remedy, you have changed something in your life (not going to the dinner) so that you are not in the reality that you don't like.

By eliminating the "shoulds" that are contributing to your unhappiness, you create a healthy sense of acceptance for what is. Let me be clear: Embracing reality does not mean condoning it. Rather, you embrace that things are the way they are, and then focus on what you can change in yourself or your environment to make reality better. You can still address the issue. For example, you can attend the holiday dinner and ask your nephew not to wear headphones at dinner because you'd like to hear about what he's been studying in school. You can even tell him his behavior has hurt your feelings in the past. Because you embrace the reality, you are willing to have a difficult conversation that might change the reality that you don't like.

There are exercises in the *Workbook* that guide you through identifying the "shoulds" in your life and developing appropriate strategies for change.

EMBRACE REALITY BY DOING BYRON KATIE'S "THE WORK"

"The Work," available for free at TheWork.com, is a process that helps you embrace reality. The first step is to recognize the ways you judge others by using Katie's "Judge Your Neighbor" worksheet. Next, you investigate your judgments using "The Four Questions":

1. Is it true?

2. Can you absolutely know it's true?

3. How do you react, what happens, when you believe that thought?

4. Who would you be without that thought?

Then you "Find the Turnarounds" for each statement, investigating whether those are true as well. For example, "My children don't listen to me" becomes "I don't listen to my children" or "My children do listen to me." Katie walks you through how to create and investigate these turnarounds.

As the last step, you learn to "Embrace Reality" by realizing and stating, for example, "I am willing to have an argument with my children because they are not listening to me."

Visit TheWork.com to practice embracing reality.

Acknowledge That Nothing Is Perfect

Another way we refuse to accept reality is by expecting people and things to be perfect. We often turn that expectation on ourselves as we try to be everything to everyone all at the same time. If you are that person trying to be perfect, I want to take a moment and give you a pat on the back and a big hug. You are awesome. You are trying really hard. No, you are not perfect, because no one is. If anyone requires that you perform perfectly, look perfect and be perfect, tell them to step down, especially if that person is yourself. Perfectionism is bad for you.

Let me repeat that: *Perfectionism is bad for you.*

Perfectionism causes psychological stress that makes us unhappy as we strive to achieve the impossible. It is bad for our health. Researchers have determined that the risks of perfectionism are as dangerous as those associated with smoking, and can cause irritable bowel disease, insomnia, heart disease, and early death. So, not only is perfection unrealistic, it is unhealthy.

Accept that nothing and no one is perfect and try the following:

1. *Be kind to yourself and others.* It's common among overachievers: You like to push yourself. It feels so productive, until you're exhausted, unhappy, and severely stressed. Give yourself a break. You're doing the best you can, right? Be kind to yourself, like you would be to others.

2. *Ask for help from your support network.* As a perfectionist, you may rarely ask for help. Why? Because you may view it as interference and also be concerned that others are judging you because you need help. But that's usually not the case. Most often, people who care about you want to help you. And one of the leading contributors to good health is a strong social network and community. Review the support network you created in the "Ask for Help" chapter, and let someone help you. It will make them feel important and take some of the pressure off you.

3. *Lay off social media.* If you are wondering why everyone else on Facebook, Twitter, Tumblr, YouTube, and Instagram seems so perfect, know this: Social media is not real life. Of course, we all know that, but do we understand how viewing all those perfectly curated posts affects us? Comparison is the thief of joy, and spending time comparing yourself to others — even when you know their social media selves are not real — can make you depressed and decrease your self-esteem. When you are looking to relax before sleep, and think "I'll just take a quick look at Facebook to wind down," don't look at your friends' posts. Instead, look at your own posts where you are having fun, spending time doing things you enjoy, and, of course, looking "perfect." Better yet, engage in some kind of mindful action like reading a book or meditating instead of engaging with social media.

4. *Save time and energy by not trying for perfection.* Aiming for perfection is costly in time, energy, and resources. And how often have you spent an inordinate amount of time trying to make something perfect, and then no one else appreciates your efforts? There is a bar above which you must operate, as a person, a spouse, a parent, an employee, a boss, and so on. But unless

you are an Olympian, perfection is usually not necessary. Do a good job, be proud of yourself for that, and pat yourself on the back for the amount of time and energy you saved by not trying to be perfect.

There are exercises in the *Workbook* to help tease out areas where you are suffering from perfectionism so you can be deliberate and mindful in banishing it from your daily life.

Keep Your Sense of Humor

After you've accepted the reality of your life and the people in it, and the fact that you and your life will never be perfect, remember to not take it all so seriously. Often, things are funny when we look back on them, even when they were not funny when they were happening. As you are living your life, go ahead and laugh about things in the moment, rather than wait until later.

Even though laughter is one of the best stress relievers, laughing in the moment can be really hard. Some circumstances in life, especially epic failures, just aren't funny.

For me, one of the biggest failures in my life was the failure of my marriage. When a marriage falls apart, the process of divorce is heavy and serious and not at all funny. But even during those difficult months, I found times to laugh, maybe not about the divorce directly, but about things related to it. For example, while we were going through the divorce, I was planning a *family* vacation to The Wizarding World of Harry Potter at Universal Studios in Orlando. We had promised our daughter we would take this family trip before we decided to divorce, and I didn't want her to miss out on it just because her parents couldn't stay married anymore. I could have viewed it as annoying to include my soon-to-be-ex-husband in our plans. Instead, I focused on how ridiculous it was that we would be spending all day, every day for a full week together, just a few short months after our divorce would be finalized!

Whatever your circumstances, try to use laughter to lighten the load so that you can better handle tough times. Nothing works more quickly than laughter to bring the mind back into balance.

Remember to have fun and laugh.

"'Should' No More" Review

1. Accept what is, especially when you cannot control the circumstance, process, or outcome.

2. Banish the "shoulds."

3. If you can control the circumstance, process, or outcome, work with the difficult reality to find a remedy.

4. If you can't control the circumstance, process, or outcome, then the remedy is to change something in yourself or your life so you don't remain in that difficult reality.

5. Accept that nothing and no one is perfect.

6. Stop perfectionism by being kind to yourself and others, allowing others to help you, laying off social media, and not aiming for perfection.

7. Keep your sense of humor.

PART 4

PRACTICE

Everything in life worth achieving requires practice.
In fact, life itself is nothing more than
one long practice session,
an endless effort of refining our motions.
– Thomas M. Sterner

KEEP TRYING: PERFECTION NOT REQUIRED

One thing is constant:
change.

When I'm not writing, I practice law. Lawyers don't "do" law, they "practice" it. The reason is that the rules and circumstances change. So even if a lawyer knows "everything" there is to know, as the laws and facts continue to change, the lawyer must continue to learn and adapt and change her approach. This practice is necessary. The same is true of life, which continues to change so that we must continue to learn and adapt and change.

As you approach and incorporate all the tools, tips, and techniques in this book into your daily life, remember it is all practice. You will not get to a point one day where you can say, "Now I've done it. I don't need to do this stuff anymore. I've accomplished it." No, rather it will be a daily practice, and what works one year may not work the next because your circumstances — or even you — will have changed. You will adapt and continue to practice.

Practice Is a Process, Not a Goal

When my daughter was seven years old, she said to me, "You don't need to keep going to yoga; you already know how to do it." Thank you, was my first thought, for acknowledging that I am a yogi, but it missed the point. Yoga is a practice. We don't master it — we grow with it and in it. The same is true of the choices, actions, and thoughts in this book. Thus, your goal will be to practice them every day, not to achieve them once and for all time.

In his amazing book *The Practicing Mind*, Thomas M. Sterner writes that we need to approach life with a childlike attitude. When we are little kids, everything is new and challenging. When we learn to walk, we try, we fall, we get back up. Sometimes we cry and seek out comfort from caregivers. Then we try again, and again, and again. Each time we learn a little more as we continue to practice and adapt and improve. When we are adults and have children, we encourage them to practice, to not be discouraged when they cannot immediately master something.

My daughter was diagnosed with dyslexia in second grade. She was an average reader, but the task of reading was exhausting for her. While she was relieved to learn there was a scientific reason that reading is challenging for her, the diagnosis didn't make the process of reading any easier. As her biggest fan and cheerleader, I tell her the process will be more difficult for her than kids who don't have dyslexia. I tell her it will require more practice and patience. Most importantly, I tell her she will be able to read, that it will get better, and that she can do it. I know those things to be true without a doubt. If someone you love has faced a similar challenge, you likely felt the same way.

We need to follow our own advice. Practice. Learn from practice. Enjoy the process. It will get better. At the very least, we will get better at practicing.

Give Yourself a Break

Give yourself a break when you don't live up to your own expectations. You are doing the best you can in the circumstances, all the time. No, you don't want to snap at your daughter when she pushes your buttons, but sometimes you will. Yes, you want to exercise four times each week, but sometimes you won't. Whatever you do, do your best, and when you don't, try again. There's always tomorrow.

Include Your Family in Your Practice

As you practice the choices, actions, and thoughts in this book, consider including your family. Children in particular benefit greatly from mindfulness and meditation. They may not be interested at first, thinking that it is boring to sit and be quiet, but once they start to feel the benefits, they will be hooked.

A good way to get started is with a book called *A Handful of Quiet: Happiness in Four Pebbles* by Thich Nhat Hanh. It describes and guides readers through a meditation practice centering around four pebbles. You start with the adventure of finding the four pebbles of your choice to represent flower (love), mountain (compassion), water (joy), and space (inclusiveness). The meditation pages in the book make it a fun game for the entire family to do together. Another beautifully illustrated picture book to introduce mindfulness to kids is *What Does It Mean to Be Present?* by Rana DiOrio and illustrated by Eliza Wheeler.

Conclusion: Live a Deliberate Life

I hope you have used this book as a helpful resource on your journey to living the time of your life. My hope for you is that you have made deliberate choices and crafted a present and future that is meaningful to you and the people you love. Keep an open mind as you journey through this life, as things change. Come back to this book any time you need to reconnect with the choices, actions, and thoughts, and remember the tools, tips, and techniques. Use *The Lawyer, the Lion, & the Laundry Workbook* to explore guided daily practices to keep you on track. There are also related tools, like the daily Practice Cards, available at www.JamieSpannhake.com.

Most importantly, remember to keep trying, and that perfection is not required.

ABOUT THE AUTHOR

Jamie Jackson Spannhake is a lawyer, writer, mediator, speaker, and certified health coach. Her work has appeared in print and online, including *Law Practice* magazine, Attorney at Work, Health Food Radar, eHow.com, Law Practice Today, The Complete Lawyer, and Electronically In Touch. She has also published in *The Brooklyn Journal of International Law* and *The Cumberland Law Review*, both academic journals. She regularly writes and speaks on issues important to women and lawyers, including time and stress management, health and wellness, and work-life integration.

She graduated magna cum laude from Brooklyn Law School and received her certification as a health coach from the Institute for Integrative Nutrition in New York City. She practices law as a partner at Berlandi Nussbaum & Reitzas LLP, as the only female partner in the firm, serving clients in Connecticut and New York in the areas of commercial litigation, estate planning, real estate, and business transactions.

In addition to writing and managing her law and mediation practice, she mothers a wonderful and happy eight-year-old daughter, successfully co-parents with her ex-husband, loves two dogs and two cats, parents foster kids, and is partially responsible for her aging parents. Even with those responsibilities, she volunteers at her daughter's school, regularly practices yoga and meditation, plays tennis, and runs several miles three to four times each week.

She is enjoying her life, without feeling exhausted or overwhelmed (though she sometimes has days when she is tired).

ACKNOWLEDGMENTS

A big thank you to an entire team of people who helped make this book possible. First, to my daughter, Sarah, for your wisdom beyond your years, your quick wit and never-ending sense of humor, and your undying love. You are my everything.

Thank you to:

Briana Ball for all things design and branding and marketing; you are a genius.

Tal Fagin and Cindy Farrar Spannhake for reading and providing excellent and insightful feedback.

Coco Sellman, Barrie Birge, and Lindsey Turner for your invaluable wisdom and direction.

Lindsey Victoria Photography for your magical photographs and advice on branding and marketing.

Sal Lopes and Pilar DeMann for making me look beautiful.

Amy Julia Becker for recommendations and knowledge in a world that you know well.

Jennifer Grant for editing and developmental commentary that helped shape this book.

My wonderful group of women friends and other mamas who "get it" and for encouraging me to continue this project that seemed to go on forever!

My Parenting Unplugged groupies and leader Tal Fagin, who are the WMS mamas (and one daddy) that let me talk, cry, vent, and laugh through it all; thank you for sharing your infinite wisdom and experience.

Joan Feldman, Mark Feldman, Joy White, and Attorney at Work for your support of my writing, your thoughtful editing, and for getting over the finish line.

Valley Spirit Wellness Center and Cooperative, Kristin Kunhardt, and Jampa Stewart for allowing us to use their magical space for a photo shoot, and for providing a safe space giving respite to many from the chaos of our world.

Marty's Café for its delicious coffee and goodies, owner Blane Withers for allowing us to use his beautiful space for a photo shoot, and Barb Jackson for facilitating it for me.

Gunn Memorial Library for allowing me to use their space for photos, writing, and brainstorming.

9 Main, for always serving up a great breakfast and cup of coffee that enabled me to work and brainstorm for this project.

Also to my mentors, who don't know me personally but who have taught me so much: Brené Brown, Brendon Burchard, Pema Chödrön, Elizabeth Gilbert, Rachel Hollis, Byron Katie, Marie Kondo, Cyndi Lee, Kate Northrup, Tony Robbins, and Thomas M. Sterner.

And to you all — your openness and support are greatly appreciated. xo

REFERENCES
& RESOURCES

S ome of the tools and techniques in this book were first published at Attorney at Work, www.attorneyatwork.com, and originally written for the benefit of lawyers. They have been edited here for a more general audience, and are reprinted with permission from Attorney at Work. Regarding the following resources, I have read (or listened to) each of these books and used each resource. I regularly update the list of resources on my website and blog.

Books

Ahlers, Amy & Arylo, Christine. *Reform Your Inner Mean Girl: 7 Steps to Stop Bullying Yourself and Start Loving Yourself* (Atria Books/Beyond Words, 2015).

Aron, Elaine N. *The Highly Sensitive Person: How to Thrive When the World Overwhelms You* (Harmony, 1997).

Bernstein, Andrew. *The Myth of Stress: Where Stress Really Comes From and How to Live a Happier and Healthier Life* (Atria Books, 2010).

Brach, Tara. *Radical Acceptance: Embracing Your Life with the Heart of a Buddha* (Bantam, 2004).

Brown, Brené. *Braving the Wilderness: The Quest for True Belonging and the Courage to Stand Alone* (Random House, 2017).

Brown, Brené. *Daring Greatly: How the Courage to Be Vulnerable Transforms the Way We Live, Love, Parent, and Lead* (Avery, 2012).

Brown, Brené. *The Gifts of Imperfection: Let Go of Who You Think You're Supposed to Be and Embrace Who You Are* (Hazelden Publishing, 2010).

Brown, Brené. *The Gifts of Imperfect Parenting: Raising Children with Courage, Compassion, and Connection* (Sounds True, 2013).

Brown, Brené. *I Thought It Was Just Me (But It Wasn't): Making the Journey from "What Will People Think?" to "I Am Enough"* (Avery, 2007).

Brown, Brené. *The Power of Vulnerability: Teachings on Authenticity, Connection, & Courage* (Sounds True, 1994).

Brown, Brené. *Rising Strong: How the Ability to Reset Transforms the Way We Live, Love, Parent, and Lead* (Random House, 2015).

Brown, Brené. *Rising Strong as a Spiritual Practice* (Sounds True, 2017).

Burns, David D. & Beck, Aaron T. *Feeling Good: The New Mood Therapy* (William Morrow Paperbacks, 1999).

Chapman, Gary. *The 5 Love Languages: The Secret to Love that Lasts* (Northfield Publishing, 2014).

Chödrön, Pema. *Comfortable with Uncertainty: 108 Teachings on Cultivating Fearlessness and Compassion* (Shambhala Publications, 2002).

Chödrön, Pema. *The Wisdom of No Escape and the Path of Loving-Kindness* (Element Books, 2004) (first published 1991).

Chödrön, Pema. *The Pocket Pema Chödrön* (Shambhala Publications, 2008).

Coelho, Paul. *The Alchemist* (Harper Collins, 1993).

Covey, Stephen R. *The 7 Habits of Highly Effective People* (Free Press, 2004) (first published 1989).

Crenshaw, Dave. *The Power of Having Fun: How Meaningful Breaks Help You Get More Done and Feel Fantastic* (Berrett-Koehler Publishers, 2017).

Duhigg, Charles. *The Power of Habit: Why We Do What We Do in Life and Business* (Random House, 2014).

Feiler, Bruce. *The Secrets of Happy Families: Improve Your Mornings, Tell Your Family History, Fight Smarter, Go Out and Play, and Much More* (William Morrow, 2013).

Ferriss, Timothy. *The 4-Hour Workweek: Escape 9-5, Live Anywhere, and Join the New Rich* (Harmony, 2007).

Fisher, Roger & Ury, William, with Patton, Bruce. *Getting to Yes: Negotiating Agreement Without Giving In* (2nd edition) (Penguin Books, 1991).

Gilbert, Elizabeth. *Big Magic: Creative Living Beyond Fear* (Riverhead Books, 2015).

Gladwell, Malcolm. *Blink: The Power of Thinking Without Thinking* (Back Bay Books, 2007).

Gladwell, Malcolm. *Outliers: The Story of Success* (Little, Brown & Co., 2008).

Gladwell, Malcolm. *The Tipping Point: How Little Things Can Make a Big Difference* (Back Bay Books, 2002).

Goleman, Daniel. *Focus: The Hidden Driver of Excellence* (Harper, 2013).

Hanson, Rick & Mendius, Richard. *Buddha's Brain: The Practical Neuroscience of Happiness, Love & Wisdom* (New Harbinger Publications, 2009).

Harris, Dan. *10% Happier: How I Tamed the Voice in My Head, Reduced Stress Without Losing My Edge, and Found Self-Help that Actually Works — A True Story* (It Books, 2014).

Helgoe, Laurie. *Introvert Power: Why Your Inner Life Is Your Hidden Strength* (Sourcebooks, 2008).

Hill, Napoleon. *Think and Grow Rich* (Ballantine Books, 1987) (updated edition published by Tarcherperigee, 2005).

His Holiness the Dali Lama XIV & Cutler, Howard C. *The Art of Happiness* (Riverhead Books, 1998).

Hollis, Rachel. *Girl, Wash Your Face: Stop Believing the Lies about Who You Are So You Can Become Who You Were Meant to Be* (Thomas Nelson, 2018).

Hollis, Rachel. *Girl, Stop Apologizing: A Shame-Free Plan for Embracing and Achieving Your Goals* (Harper Collins, 2019).

Katie, Byron. *Loving What Is: Four Questions That Can Change Your Life* (Harmony, 2003).

Keller, Gary & Papasan, Jay. *The One Thing: The Surprisingly Simple Truth Behind Extraordinary Results* (Bard Press, 2013).

Kiyosaki, Robert T. *Rich Dad Poor Dad: What the Rich Teach Their Kids About Money — That the Poor and Middle Class Do Not!* (Warner Books, 1997) (updated 2nd edition published in 2017).

Klein, Allen. *Secrets Kids Know that Adults Oughta Learn: Enrich Your Life by Viewing It Through the Eyes of a Child* (Viva Editions, 2017).

Kondo, Marie. *The Life-Changing Magic of Tidying Up: The Japanese Art of Decluttering and Organizing* (Ten Speed Press, 2014).

Kozak, Arnie. *The Everything Essential Buddhism Book: A Guide to the Fundamental Beliefs and Traditions of Buddhism, Past and Present* (Simon & Schuster, 2015).

Krans, Kim. *The Wild Unknown Animal Spirit Deck & Guidebook* (Harper Elixir, 2018).

Lahey, Jessica. *The Gift of Failure: How the Best Parents Learn to Let Go so Their Children Can Succeed* (Harper, 2015).

Lee, Cyndi. *May I Be Happy: A Memoir of Love, Yoga, and Changing My Mind* (Dutton, 2013).

Lee, Cyndi. *Yoga Body, Buddha Mind: A Complete Manual for Physical and Spiritual Well-Being from the Founder of the Om Yoga Center* (Riverhead Books, 2004).

Northrup, Kate. *Do Less: Revolutionary Approach to Time and Energy Management for Busy Moms* (Hay House, 2019).

Northrup, Kate. *Money, A Love Story: Untangle Your Financial Woes and Create the Life You Really Want* (Hay House, 2013).

Peck, M. Scott. *The Road Less Traveled: A New Psychology of Love, Traditional Values, and Spiritual Growth* (Touchstone, 2003: 25th Anniversary edition) (first published by Simon & Schuster, 1978).

Price, Catherine. *Gratitude: A Journal* (Chronicle Books, 2009).

Rath, Tom. *Strengths Finder 2.0* (Gallup Press, 2007).

Redfield, James. *The Celestine Prophecy: An Adventure* (Warner Books, 1997).

Robbins, Tony. *Awaken the Giant Within: How to Take Immediate Control of Your Mental, Emotional, Physical and Financial Destiny!* (Free Press, 1992).

Robbins, Tony. *Unlimited Power: The New Science of Personal Achievement* (Free Press, 1997).

Rubin, Gretchen. *The Happiness Project: Or, Why I Spent a Year Trying to Sing in the Morning, Clean My Closets, Fight Right, Read Aristotle, and Generally Have More Fun* (Harper, 2009).

Steiner, Claude & Perry, Paul. *Achieving Emotional Literacy: A Personal Program to Increase Your Emotional Intelligence* (Avon Books, 1997).

Sterner, Thomas M. *The Practicing Mind: Developing Focus and Discipline in Your Life — Master Any Skill or Challenge by Learning to Love the Process* (Mountain Sage, 2006).

Warren, Rick. *The Purpose Driven Life: What on Earth Am I Here For?* (Zondervan Publishing, 2007).

Children's Books & Resources

Coombs, Kate & Laitinen, Anna Emilia. *Breathe and Be: A Book of Mindfulness Poems* (Sounds True, 2017).

DiOrio, Rana & Wheeler, Eliza. *What Does It Mean to Be Present?* (Little Pickle Stories, 2010).

Hanh, Thich Nhat. *A Handful of Quiet: Happiness in Four Pebbles* (Plum Blossom Books, 2012).

Little Pickle Press, whose mission is to create media that fosters kindness in young people: www.littlepicklepress.com.

Plum Blossom Books, which publishes books on mindfulness for young people and the grown-ups in their lives: www.parallax.org.

Audiobooks

Many of the books I've listed above I listened to using one of the apps below. There are also a few books that are only audiobooks, available as "Audible Originals."

Audible.com: www.audible.com.

Hoopla app (if your public library utilizes it): www.hoopladigital.com.

Libby app (if your public library utilizes it): https://meet.libbyapp.com.

Overdrive app (if your public library utilizes it): https://app.overdrive.com.

It's Not What It Looks Like, by Molly Burke (an Audible original) (Audible, 2019). Available for free with Audible account or free trial at https//www.audible.com/pd/Its-Not-What-It-Looks-Like-Audiobook/B07TVF9RMY.

The Man on the Mountaintop, by Susan Trott (an Audible original) (Audible, 2017). Available for free with Audible account or free trial at https://www.audible.com/pd/The-Man-on-the-Mountaintop-Audiobook/B075Y4SWJ8.

New Family Values, by Andrew Soloman (an Audible original) (Audible, 2018). Available for free with Audible account or free trial at https://www.audible.com/pd/New-Family-Values-Audiobook/B07KCPR91G.

Meditation and Mindfulness

21 Days of Meditation, by Aaptiv, available at Audible.com for subscribers. Available for free with Audible account or free trial at https://www.audible.com/pd/21-Days-of-Meditation-Audiobook/B07LBXPKZ5.

Headspace app: contains a great beginner's 10-day guided meditation program called "Basics"; requires a subscription to continue using it after completing the "Basics." Available at www.headspace.com.

Let's Meditate app: free guided meditations of varying durations that can be downloaded for offline use.

Stop, Breathe & Think: Meditation and Mindfulness app: free guided meditations of varying durations; each session starts with a check-in on how your feel physically, mentally, and emotionally so the app can make recommendations on which meditations would be helpful. Available at www.stopbreathethink.com.

Cyndi Lee: www.cyndilee.com (meditation courses, training, and information).

Thich Nhat Hahn Foundation: thichnhathanhfoundation.org (Escondido, California).

Valley Spirit Wellness Center and Cooperative: www.valleyspiritcoop.com (Washington, Connecticut).

Zen Buddhism: Simple Wisdom for Happy Living: www.zen-buddhism.net.

Yoga

Cyndi Lee: www.cyndilee.com (yoga courses, training, and information).

Down Dog app: www.downdogapp.com.

Pocket Yoga app: www.pocketyoga.com.

Valley Spirit Wellness Center and Cooperative: www.valleyspiritcoop.com (Washington, Connecticut).

YogaTX, on YouTube: https://www.youtube.com/user/yogatx.

Yoga with Adrienne: https://yogawithadriene.com; and on YouTube: https://www.youtube.com/user/yogawithadriene.

Fitness

Daily Workout apps: http://dailyworkoutapps.com.

FitBit and FitBit app (wearable fitness tracker and app to log your fitness goals, including sleep, exercise, weight, and more). Available at www.fitbit.com.

MindBody app (to find fitness, wellness, and beauty classes and services in your area, including yoga, meditation, massage, and more). Available at www.mindbodyonline.com.

MyFitnessPal app (food journal and database with informational blog, including recipes). Available at www.myfitnesspal.com.

Retreats and Events

Kripalu Center for Yoga and Health: www.kripalu.org (Stockbridge, Massachusetts).

Omega Institute for Holistic Health: www.eomega.org (Rhinebeck, New York).

Valley Spirit Wellness Center and Cooperative: www.valleyspiritcoop.com (Washington, Connecticut).

Websites and Services

Chewy.com: for all pet items and needs.

IntegrativeNutrition.com: lots of useful information on health, wellness, and nutrition, and courses for health coach certification.

MindMeister.com: mind mapping tool for online use via computer and app. It offers a free basic plan as well as paid subscriptions for various uses, including personal, professional, and business.

StitchFix.com: for clothes, shoes, and accessories.

Tal Fagin at TalFusion, a Martha Beck-certified life coach: talfusion.net.

Tidying Up with Marie Kondo (Netflix series).

TheWork.com: Byron Katie's website with free resources and information.

And, of course, JamieSpannhake.com and AttorneyatWork.com.

MORE

Additional Support and Helpful Information

Interested in receiving more support? Visit www.JamieSpannhake.com to learn about and purchase additional support products, including *The Lawyer, the Lion, & the Laundry Workbook*, daily Practice Cards, and the Thought Book journal. You can also download worksheets, receive invaluable free resources, obtain bonus information and materials, subscribe to the blog, watch informational videos, and more.

Hire Jamie to Speak at Your Next Event or Write for Your Publication

Jamie has been speaking to groups and organizations and writing for publications for over 10 years. She's an expert on time and stress management, healthy lifestyle choices, and handling life with its competing responsibilities. She has helped countless individuals achieve a healthier balance in their lives.

Author of *The Lawyer, the Lion, & the Laundry: Three Hours to Finding Your Calm in the Chaos*, Jamie believes a great life starts with doing the hard work of clarifying your values and priorities in order to create the life you want to live. This clarity, combined with mindfulness through meditation, a useful support network, organization, an acceptance of reality, and adjusting as life changes, leads to a fulfilled life.

She has served on numerous expert panels, including for the New York City Bar Association and the American Bar Association. She regularly writes for Attorney at Work and her own blog. Her writing has appeared in *Law Practice* magazine, Law Practice Today webzine, *GP/Solo* magazine, The Complete Lawyer, Electronically In Touch, Health Food Radar, and eHow.com.

For more information or to hire Jamie for your next event or publication, visit www.JamieSpannhake.com.

Reviews

Did you enjoy this book? Please leave an honest review and feedback on Amazon, Goodreads, or elsewhere.

Follow me

Twitter: IdealYear
Facebook: LawyerLionLaundry
Instagram: lawyerlionlaundry
Pinterest: jamiejspannhake
LinkedIn: jamiespannhake
www.JamieSpannhake.com

What I Want

Live (NE)
- Welcoming community
- new open space
- Water
- access to good food
- shopping
- Somewhere I can continue to walk
- PT
- Close enough to physical/cultural resources & experiences
- beautiful & safe areas to walk/running community

career
- Work-life balance
- Instate tuition (VA)
- Job w/ reasonable hours
- Comfortable salary
- travel
- retirement

family
- live near family (NE)
- more engagement
- quality relationships or friendships
- better relationships w/ my husband, son, sister
- Nieces

time / activities
- exercise
- cook
- read
- stitch
- keep in touch w/ friends + family
- birthdays
- travel — one trip per year
- volunteer
- church
- kind

Friends
- honest
- relaxed
- sense of humor
- kind
- thoughtful

Person
- thoughtful
- supportive
- respected
- energetic
- honest
- loving
- kind

healthy
- time to exercise & to eat right
- See Dr. reg.

If only I had . . . life would be better.

easier job
more time
more $ $
lived closer to family
had friends
a better marriage
time to exercise
less stress
lived back in the NE

Made in the USA
Columbia, SC
12 December 2022

73518243R00059